CONSTELLATIONS

Like the future itself, the imaginative possibilities of science fiction are limitless. And the very development of cinema is inextricably linked to the genre, which, from the earliest depictions of space travel and the robots of silent cinema to the immersive 3D wonders of contemporary blockbusters, has continually pushed at the boundaries. **Constellations** provides a unique opportunity for writers to share their passion for science fiction cinema in a book-length format, each title devoted to a significant film from the genre. Writers place their chosen film in a variety of contexts – generic, institutional, social, historical – enabling **Constellations** to map the terrain of science fiction cinema from the past to the present... and the future.

'This stunning, sharp series of books fills a real need for authoritative, compact studies of key science fiction films. Written in a direct and accessible style by some of the top critics in the field, brilliantly designed, lavishly illustrated and set in a very modern typeface that really shows off the text to best advantage, the volumes in the **Constellations** series promise to set the standard for SF film studies in the 21st century.'
Wheeler Winston Dixon, Ryan Professor of Film Studies, University of Nebraska

 Constellations

Constelbooks

Also available in this series

12 Monkeys Susanne Kord

Blade Runner Sean Redmond

Children of Men Dan Dinello

Close Encounters of the Third Kind Jon Towlson

The Damned Nick Riddle

Inception David Carter

RoboCop Omar Ahmed

Rollerball Andrew Nette

Forthcoming

Brainstorm Joseph Maddrey

Ex Machina Joshua Grimm

Jurassic Park Paul Bullock

Mad Max Martyn Conterio

Stalker Jon Hoel

CONSTELLATIONS

D U N E

Christian McCrea

Acknowledgements

The entirety of this project is owed to Alexandra Heller-Nicholas. Her encouragement and guidance was the catalyst for both this book's inception and the fuel by which it would be written. Her books on *Suspiria* (Auteur/Devil's Advocates, 2015) and *Ms. 45* (Wallflower Press/Cultographies, 2017) were inspirations for both their uncompromising style and attention to detail.

The Australian Film Institute's Research Collection housed at RMIT University in Melbourne, Australia, headed by librarians Cathie Gillam and Alex Gionfriddo, deserves a very special thank you for a paper and material archive dating back to the film's release. The collection is an incomparable treasure.

Thanks also to Dr. Dean Brandum who deserves a special mention for box office research which constitutes the first detailed analysis of the film's exhibition trajectory; to Clare Nina Norelli for an extremely rare interview that added greatly to the passages on Lynch; to Mark Bennett at Duneinfo.com whose diligence in keeping the film's legacy alive on the website and social media has been indispensable – resources there made several passages of this film possible; to the two Orthodox Herbertarians who wish to remain anonymous for their broader picture of the series of novels and their mythos; to my colleagues at work, Helen Stuckey, Jen Lade, James Manning, Emma Witkowski, Douglas Wilson, Adam Nash and Mira Thurner; to my family, especially Fiona and Rob, Dale, Kitty and my brother Chris. Finally, thanks to all the friends both near and far who share my love of the film.

First published in 2019 by
Auteur, 24 Hartwell Crescent, Leighton Buzzard LU7 1NP
www.auteur.co.uk
Copyright © Auteur 2019

Series design: Nikki Hamlett at Cassels Design
Set by Cassels Design www.casselsdesign.co.uk

All rights reserved. No part of this publication may be reproduced in any material form (including photocopying or storing in any medium by electronic means and whether or not transiently or incidentally to some other use of this publication) without the permission of the copyright owner.

British Library Cataloguing-in-Publication Data
A catalogue record for this book is available from the British Library

ISBN paperback: 978-1-911325-82-6
ISBN ebook: 978-1-911325-**83-3**

Contents

Introduction 7

1. A Dream Unfolds: Before *Dune* 13
   Science Fiction's Many Cultures
   The Writing of *Dune*
   The Shadow of *Star Wars*
   Between *Star Wars* and *Dune* 1977-1984

2. The Weirding Way: The Makers of *Dune* 33
   House Jodorowsky and House Scott
   House De Laurentiis
   House Lynch
   The Little Makers: Cast and Crew
   All Eyes Turned to Arrakis

3. Mind in Motion: Watching *Dune* 63
   A Very Delicate Time
   Planet Kaitain
   Planet Caladan
   Planet Giedi Prime
   Folding Space
   Judging the Change
   Dune's Spiral Structure
   Planet Ellipsis
   Total and Permanent Montage
   The Final Battle

4. The Sleeper Has Awakened: After *Dune* 101
   They Tried and Died
   The Harvesters of *Dune*
   The Games of *Dune*

5. The Golden Path 115

Bibliography 118

INTRODUCTION

> David Lynch takes his turn at the microphone, pleading with the packed house of revelers to pipe down so that he can squeeze in a few words. ... A few minutes pass, and Lynch is given his moment of silence. But just as he opens his mouth, a mariachi band bursts into the room, energetically launching into a song, drowning out his words. The crowd breaks up. (Sammon 1984: 28)

January 27, 1984: The scene is a combined wrap party for Dune (David Lynch, 1984) and *Conan the Destroyer* (Richard Fleischer, 1984). Both were made at the Churubusco Studios in Mexico City, and both produced by Raffaella De Laurentiis, daughter of legendary Italian film producer Dino De Laurentiis. The anecdote above opens Paul M. Sammon's 1984 *Dune* diary in *Cinefantastique* magazine, and although Sammon may have intuited how symbolic the moment was, it's only in retrospect that it provides a microcosm of the buildup, production and release of a film often maligned as being out of step both with its genre and with its director's broader oeuvre: Lynch thought he found the perfect moment to make his big statement, but was cut off before he could say a word.

Dune emerged from the miasma of a long production as a haunting, driven, mesmerising vision of the distant future. Frank Herbert's original 1965 novel of the same name and its sequels built a meticulous universe of dark majesty and justice, wild-eyed freedom fighters and relentless authoritarians; Lynch's film adaptation would take no less than three and a half years to make, dividing critics and fans of both Lynch and Herbert alike. Or so the story goes.

Yet the film itself bursts and bellows with ancient and uncontrollable life. Bombastic, glassy-eyed characters shake the earth and dread mysteries echo off the desert sands of Arrakis. Smirking villains await their moment, and idealists fret in the dark. There are cruel mothers and distant fathers, vengeful desert gargantuans and silent, floating bullets. Intensely stark and sexual moments saunter past the PG rating like a bully pushing past a nightclub bouncer. Inevitably compared to *Star Wars* (George Lucas, 1977), *Dune* is quieter, darker and more cerebral. Voice-overs of characters' internal thoughts punctuate the drama like a bass drum.

After several attempts to produce a film – including, most famously, by the extraordinary Chilean director Alejandro Jodorowsky, as lovingly outlined in the cult documentary *Jodorowsky's Dune* (Frank Pavich, 2013) – it fell to Raffaella De Laurentiis to spearhead production of the film while Dino remained at arm's length, managing the production empire. Finally settling on Mexico City's huge Churubusco complex, Lynch and Raffaella assembled a team over the coming years to develop a film with a unique look and feel. *Dune* would eventually feature the work of a creative team drawn from several different cinema traditions and from their individual networks of collaborators.

David Lynch interviewed in Great Directors *(Angela Ismailos, 2009)*

Now routinely and unabashedly ejected from the Lynch auteur canon (including by the director himself), I argue strongly that *Dune* is nevertheless recognisably a 'Lynch film'. Interviewed for the documentary *Great Directors*, he described the process of filming and producing *Dune* as 'maybe 75 per cent nightmare', and credits it as setting him on the path of needing total directorial control on later work (Angela Ismailos, 2009). Yet *Dune* also tells a story of its own; while science fiction fan culture was polarised between horrified or amazed, Frank Herbert himself was very pleased. Broader film culture had no idea what to say at first, and the myth of a young director waylaid by the Hollywood machine provided a durable narrative. In the decades since, *Dune* has attained a symbolic place in the history of supposedly disastrous film productions, but it is regardless one whose many vocal and energetic fans refuse to forget.

The book and the film are both famous for their overly complicated plot elements, but can be summarised fairly simply with the benefit of decades of hindsight. The film centres on the plot of a great betrayal between armies, the noble families in charge of them, and the revenge taken out in its wake. Its setting is a distant future, where intergalactic travel is powered by a substance – the spice melange – which exists only on a desert planet, Arrakis. The known universe's Emperor makes a deal with the Spacing Guild, who control all interstellar travel. He is to kill young prince Paul Atreides, and they are let in on the Emperor's plan to destroy Paul's family and army with the help of a rival family, House Harkonnen. His suspicion aroused, Paul is tested by the Bene Gesserit sisterhood before travelling to Arrakis – he is powerfully prescient and might possess the qualities belonging to a prophesised messiah, the Kwisatch Haderach. His family travels to Arrakis to take over spice mining, seemingly from the ousted Harkonnen. He is introduced to the Fremen, the inhabitants of the planet, whose secretive culture seems to hide great secrets. The Emperor's plan unfolds and the Harkonnen return with a sneak attack, killing Paul's father. Paul and his mother Jessica escape to the desert and find sanctuary among the Fremen. His growing preternatural awareness and his fitting the profile of an ancient prophecy allows him to quickly become their prophesised leader, Muad'dib. He trains them in a new art of war – the weirding way – which uses sound to destroy. Once he is changed and empowered by a dangerous distillation of the spice, they tame the giant worms of Arrakis, whose relationship to the spice seems to be the most guarded secret of all. With a vast army, Paul assaults the Harkonnen and the Emperor's panicked troops with overwhelming force. Paul all but declares himself the new Emperor of the universe, and with a soft breath, summons a great rainstorm over Arrakis – confirmation that he is the Kwisatch Haderach.

The 1984 film version of *Dune* has a life all its own that lies beyond the intentions of Herbert, Lynch, the De Laurentiis family, and its myriad cast and crew. Its narrative structure, characterisations, its approach to science fiction, and audiovisual language are all highly idiosyncratic. These co-mingle and produce intense reactions in the viewer, the shock and excitement of new cinematic ideas still resonating over thirty years since the film's release. *Dune* is audaciously a science fiction film that refuses to be futuristic; a political narrative undone by the power of prophecy and dream;

an adventure story structured like a poem; a big budget blockbuster that refuses to foreground action sequences. Watching *Dune* feels like being unmoored from cinema itself, free-floating in the form's infinite, unexplored possibilities. At once religiously observant to Herbert's material but heavily reliant on its own internal logic, these elements provide the core of what I will explore throughout this book.

The first chapter maps the science fiction milieu into which Lynch's *Dune* would enter. Science fiction cinema had been bursting into new life throughout the late 1970s and early 1980s; while the first *Star Wars* trilogy loomed large, stories of interstellar science fiction were changing elsewhere, and with no small influence of Frank Herbert's original novel. His approach to fiction and personal biography provide some of the seeds of what the film would become. Since *Dune* occurs in the shadow of *Star Wars*, this chapter will also provide context for the production and consumption of science fiction film in the years between the two releases.

The second chapter tells the story of *Dune*'s production, through the lens of the film's reputation, histories and key players. After some false starts, a consortium acquired the rights and attached *El Topo* (1970) director Alejandro Jodorowsky. In their collaboration, stark, bulbous images emerged from the pen of famed French comic artist Jean 'Moebius' Giraud. A huge world-building enterprise to match Herbert's own was slowly taking shape, but also falling apart, as lovingly recalled in *Jodorowsky's Dune*. After another false start with Ridley Scott – all occurring as *Star Wars* was changing the landscape – the project sparked to life with the arrival of David Lynch, fresh off of the success of the Academy Award-nominated *The Elephant Man* (1980). Lynch's reputation before and since are part of *Dune*'s story; especially how the film sits both inside and outside a canonical view of his work.

In the third chapter, we travel to *Dune* proper and explore one of science fiction's strangest outliers. Examining the impressive cast, the lurid set designs, and the spiralling dialogue exchanges, this chapter charts the film's internal logic through key shots and scenes with reference to Herbert's notes, Lynch's scripts, and the much-discussed and controversial 'Alan Smithee' television edit of the film, as well as considering a range of critical and academic responses. Finally, in the last chapter we examine the perhaps unexpected longevity of a film that was for many deemed dead on arrival. From absurd tie-in merchandise to incredible comic translations to the videogames that changed game history in significant ways, I assess the film's lasting legacy.

Across this book, I emphasise how Lynch's *Dune* demands our attention like no other film; it unfolds ceremonially into a dream already in motion. In the history of science fiction cinema, it remains a focussed, singular vision that startles and delights in its difference. It represents every dashed hope and upraised hand of anguish that believed *Dune*'s literary universe could be adapted given the right conditions. As the armies of different grand houses vie for control of the desert planet Arrakis, so have competing writers, directors, producers, fans and critics all looked to mine the setting's deep promise. It represents so much to so many in search of parables of failure, promise, corrupt systems and ineffable creative possibility – the magic dust in the desert.

I. A DREAM UNFOLDS: BEFORE *DUNE*

With David Lynch's unambiguous ejection of the film from his oeuvre, *Dune* is an orphan. Likewise, it sits both inside and outside the science fiction film canon because, for many, it represents film's inability to translate science fiction literature. So where does *Dune* belong? Its mediocre reception in 1984 ensured it was considered a failure at a time when blockbuster high-concept cinema was in full swing and new, brash sci-fi subgenres were packing in audiences. Lynch's next film, *Blue Velvet* (1986) returned him to accolades, critical acclaim and – most importantly for him – granted him an increasing license for creative freedom than major movie productions would usually allow. It has therefore been tempting for critics to retrospectively describe *Dune* as a struggle between a director and the material he tried to adapt: this temptation, I argue, is part of the myth-making around the film – a project that was in terms of Lynch at first everybody's treasure and then nobody's fault.

Long before the film, Frank Herbert's 1965 novel shook the science fiction landscape with a blistering and exacting parable of a boy on the verge of a galaxy-spanning mistake; fulfilling the prophecy of overturning the order of the cosmos. The nature of the novel, while evocative, sparingly uses deep visual descriptions and frequently inserts deep background information. With this in mind, only a couple of years after the film's release, Universal set about re-editing some of the cut material back into *Dune*, and inserted a long spoken prologue over paintings of new characters and environments. This version was intended to make the film more palatable for television, but was immediately disowned by Lynch, for whom it surely was salt in the wound of not having final cut on the film. Commonly referred to as the 1988 Extended Edition, this book will make reference to this version as 'The Alan Smithee version'.[1]

While the existence of this version disgusted Lynch, it expanded the film's audience considerably and marked the beginnings of its rehabilitation in the various science fiction cultures that had no idea how to reconcile its mood, tone and aesthetics with the density and deep promise of the Herbert universe. Several fan edits continued to appear well into the twenty-first century, tinkering with the insertion of cut footage, the order of events, voice-over material, and the controversial painted introduction of the Alan Smithee version. *Dune* Redux. *Dune* Perfected. *Dunes* Without End.

Director title card for the 1984 Dune *and the later Alan Smithee cut*

The film's reception also left a door open for future attempts to further develop the Herbert material. For Philip Strick, 'Herbert left appearances mostly to the imagination. Much of the millions spent over the years on developing his work have been devoted not to the script but to the setting, an endless gallery of dream palaces, twin-mooned landscapes and exotic costumes' (2001: 20). This quote appeared in a review of the first of two mini-series made for the Sci-Fi Channel, cheekily called *Frank Herbert's Dune* (2001) and *Frank Herbert's Children of Dune* (2003) to signal their return to the original novels. *Frank Herbert's Dune* was especially well done, held together by a stately William Hurt, but it also didn't scratch the itch in the same way as Lynch's version had: the universe seemed grander, but somehow less felt at stake. *Children of Dune* expanded the universe at breakneck pace and brought much of the drama back to the personal scale. The sense of history and scale were stronger in the mini-series format, but the arch alchemy of Lynch's version had been traded away. There was no danger or thrill here, but rather calm, clinical and well-paced drama that won Emmys.

At the time of writing, French-Canadian director Denis Villeneuve – having completed two big-budget science fiction films in *Arrival* (2016) and *Blade Runner 2049* (2017) – had begun developing a new version of *Dune* which he has repeatedly promised would be different to Lynch's. In 2017, he said that 'I'm going back to the book, and going to the images that came out when I read it' (Villeneuve, quoted by Yahoo! Movies: 2017). What becomes of Villeneuve's version cannot be guessed at this point, but what is of note is that the Alan Smithee version, the Sci-Fi Channel mini-series and Villeneuve's future adaptation all privilege a return to the original Herbert text – that is their shared unimpeachable, incorruptible quest.

So here we enter our first paradox. Why was Herbert himself so happy with the Lynch film which other directors and producers have since sought to correct? Lynch's *Dune* doesn't attempt to just adapt the Herbert material; it *dreams* in it. Otherwise simple plots compress and expand as characters share their fears and voice their ambiguities. Where other sci-fi epics had good-natured robots and friendly banter, *Dune* takes time out to reveal stark, intense dream sequences and ominous declarations. In this pre-history, I travel to the different worlds of science fiction cinema and literature to consider how Frank Herbert's *Dune* changed the landscape of science fiction. I peer into the shadow that *Star Wars* cast over the production environment, and the effect this would have on Lynch's imagining of Herbert's novel.

SCIENCE FICTION'S MANY CULTURES

Surrounding Lynch's *Dune* is a whole cosmos of questions and issues surrounding the meanings and value of science fiction itself – context for why the book was so important, and why the film represented so much both in its build-up and then public failure. One of the enduring traits of science fiction culture is that it doesn't really *endure* as such at all. Rather, groups of fans, self-organising into different groups and categories, react with intense creativity to a particular film, series or book. Often, this group will not cross over as openly and obviously as those outside science fiction culture might expect. Fans constellate, cluster, and cohere in ways which might make sense to a sociologist: there's been sci-fi conventions since before the dawn of television. Yet what's most interesting isn't just how sci-fi fans behave and what they believe in, but how they differ from other genre-centric fan cultures. For Angela Ndalianis, science fiction television in particular makes passionate fans: 'The conditions, secret ingredients and magic potions that generate the cult experience can be dramatically amplified by the serial logic of television' (Ndalianis 2011: 63).

Some of these 'conditions [and] secret ingredients' are often as simple as the narrative tropes of repetition, delay, and return – of characters, places and things. The pay-off for a dedicated fan of a particular sci-fi universe can often feel like a win at a casino or opening a paycheque. You are, after all, 'cashing in' built-up prior knowledge when the show or film makes a reveal, re-introduces an old character, or repeats a beloved trope or refrain. Partially because so much of the surface pleasure of science fiction is the new (mostly futuristic) objects, places and technologies which require just enough description to spark imagination, your relationship with that universe as a whole has already exceeded the boundaries you've been given: at first meeting, you're *already* thinking about the lightsaber that belongs to the boy's father, and wondering what it can cut. You're *already* thinking about the transporter beam and what it could do to water, to torpedoes, to people. You're *already* thinking about the spice melange, and how it transforms everyone it touches.

Perhaps it is because of this formula – *mise-en-scène* acquires curiosity, curiosity acquires knowledge, knowledge becomes a habit – that science fiction is resolutely about its universes more than it is about its intellectual properties, franchises or even media. That single word 'universes' is more instructive, descriptive and relevant because it tells us how open-ended yet absolutely disconnected from itself science fiction is, how it works, and what it means to people. While a science fiction fan will watch all kinds of science fiction, scratch the surface and that habitual deep knowledge will show. Science fiction has a constellation of fandoms that move and interconnect. Science fiction is not one culture but many cultures; *Dune* is one of these.

Herbert himself seemed aware of this. A 1981 interview ventures into social poetry with commentary that people use 'the rich world of other people's imagination for their own escape' from their alienation, 'seeking answers in the artful and ingenious worlds of the future' (Rovner 1981). The genre is expressive of *art and ingenuity* in very real terms – designs of places, people and things that lie just beyond a premise. This is not 'escapism' – a term with ample vernacular power but that has perhaps lost its ability to produce deep critical reading. The pleasure taken in spectating science fiction's art and ingenuity is something more concrete and real, almost a physical experience, or an experience with matter itself. This allows us to see science fiction's special effects and the narrative and thematic tones of the genre as far less separate and more interconnected. They're bonded through their treatment of *matter*. Science fiction is an invitation to speculate. This animating spirit – as much scientism as escapism – accurately describes the *Dune* universe. We're fascinated by the characters but the spice melange is central to the story, and to our capacity to speculate on it.

On this theme, Ursula LeGuin wrote a short essay 'A Non-Euclidean View of California as a Cold Place to Be' that riffs off Thomas More's famous fifteenth-century religious satire *Utopia*. LeGuin says that the utopian impulse is 'pure structure without content; pure model; goal. That is its virtue. Utopia is uninhabitable' (2016: 166). Disappointment and delay are as much the long cultural business of science fiction as spectacle, revelation and adolescent relishes of fantasy and power. In another short piece collected in the same volume alongside the original Thomas More essay, LeGuin distinguishes between types of utopian impulses; a 'utopiyin' and a 'utopiyang', both different versions of 'a blueprint without a building site' (2016: 195). For LeGuin, her adaptation of the Chinese metonymic concepts translates to 'Yang is control, yin acceptance. They are great and equal powers; neither can exist alone, and each is always in process of becoming the other' (2016: 196).[2]

As science fiction developed different audiences throughout the twentieth century in literature, film, television and comics, the universes multiplied but their relationship to each other and their individual styles also became more complex. They were both in dialogue and disagreement. From this were produced some profoundly interesting splits: Hard science fiction literature (stories which are deeply rooted in rationally proposed scientific fact) vs. soft science fiction (which focus on social questions). To the outsider, this would seem to map to more prosaic and pop-culture faux-debate fan fodder such as *Star Trek* vs. *Star Wars*. But in retrospect, these splits are highly functional; they not only provoke audiences but also inspire new productions through the nearly intangible genres of inspiration and reference that weave through creative history. This also applied to scholarship as much as film and television; in *Science-Fiction Cinema: From Outerspace To Cyberspace*, Geoff King and Tanya Kryswinska explain that 'social-cultural and industrial perspectives are sometimes divergent, providing different explanations for the same phenomena, but sometimes mutually reinforcing' as they set about exploring the range of different science fiction film scholarship they were working with (2000: 3).

Of all the writing about film science fiction during the latter half of the twentieth century, what is notable in retrospect is how aware all sorts of people – writers, fans, critics, directors – were about the changes that computer mediated imagery would bring to science fiction itself. Brooks Landon wrote in 1992 about a coming wave of cyberpunk film, in which the conflict between humans and computers will be recast 'as a conflict of personalities within the computer-generated worlds of cyberspace' (1992: 137). Much of the second half of his book *The Aesthetics of Ambivalence* positions the looming changes stemming from computer culture not just as the orientation of future science fiction cinema, but where so much had already been oriented. Landon voiced in academic terms what fans had known instinctually; that special effects are never *just* special effects, and spectacle is never *just* spectacle. They serve a purpose that is quintessential to science fiction; to orient the eye and mind towards imaginative work. This is no small linguistic pinprick, and it's crucial as we go back and consider Lynch's approach to *Dune*.

Elsewhere, the social picture of science fiction was coming increasingly into view. Coinciding with the early Internet, science fiction studies such as Annette Kuhn's edited collection *Alien Zone: Cultural Theory and Contemporary Science-Fiction Cinema* (1990) were framing the changes within the genre as they were happening. There, H. Bruce Franklin wrote about Hollywood science fiction between 1970 and 1982 and noted that 'by the end of the 1960s, it seemed we were experiencing the most profound crisis in human history', framing the early 80s as a moment of paradoxical social relief, reflected in the changes in science fiction narratives (1990:

19). In 1978, Joan Dean seemed to presage this somewhat by outlining how the gap in time between *2001: A Space Odyssey* (Stanley Kubrick, 1968) and *Star Wars* is as important as their respective creative and mass cultural importance – appearing within a lull where little of value was (in her opinion) otherwise produced (1978: 32-41).

Of course, science fiction cinema was thriving on its own terms, co-mingling with horror, thriller, and social satire in films like *Silent Running* (Douglas Trumbull 1972), *Dark Star* (John Carpenter, 1974), *Soylent Green* (Richard Fleischer, 1973) and non-Hollywood films like *The Man Who Fell to Earth* (Nicolas Roeg, 1976) and *Solaris* (Andrei Tarkovsky, 1972) which were also making critical waves. Science fiction fans were also well served by the small screen; American television series such as *Space: 1999* (1975-1977) and *The Six Million Dollar Man* (1973-1978) and British series like *Doomwatch* (1970-1972) and *Blake's 7* (1978-1981) were provoking and reacting to quite different audience cultures, in a time when it was less likely for crossover national audiences to emerge. If, as Ndalianis points out, television science fiction uses the serial logic of the form to provoke cult engagement, then seriality was about to intrude on science fiction in more ways than one; not just in terms of the obvious fictional universes and film series, but also in terms of clear, definable, digestible Hollywood genres via the blockbuster impact to come.

THE WRITING OF DUNE

Frank Herbert had been steadily writing science fiction short stories for magazines for some time before the publication of his first novel, *The Dragon in the Sea* (1956) which adapted a serialised story that appeared in *Astounding* magazine the preceding year. During this time, Herbert was a journalist for newspapers like the *Oregon Statesmen* and *Seattle Star*, and an editor for the *California Living* magazine in the *San Francisco Examiner*. Six months as a Navy photographer had produced some inspiration for *The Dragon in the Sea*, where the world is sharply divided between West and East forces. The West, which uses submarines to steal oil from the East, has recently found that its submarines have been disappearing. The psychological terror and tension of the 'subtug' crews are the focus of the mystery.

In one of Herbert's earlier stories, 'Looking for Something' in the April 1952 issue of *Startling Stories*, a hypnotist is on the verge of discovering that the world he knows is a grand hypnotic illusion. A vast alien conspiracy exists to farm humans for a glandular secretion; the same kind of paranoid global ruse premise that would later influence *The Matrix* (The Wachowskis, 1999). In another, 'Operation Syndrome', published in the June 1954 issue of *Astounding*, a plague-like outbreak of madness is destroying whole cities. Protagonist Dr. Eric Ladde is working on a device that will end the outbreak, and one night, he dreams of a beautiful woman who sings for him, who turns out to be part of the cause of the crisis. While the story wasn't a direct influence on Lynch's *Eraserhead* (1977) – which drew on both Nikolai Gogol's story 'The Nose' (1836) and Kafka's 1915 novella *Metamorphosis* – that film also coincidentally featured a mysterious beautiful singer, a human beam of light at the centre of the corruption (Olson 2008: 54). Various iterations of this figure would repeat in Lynch's work, such as *Blue Velvet*, *Twin Peaks* (1990–1991), and *Mulholland Drive*.

Herbert's thematic concerns before *Dune* were already tending towards the ecological and political. Having worked as a reporter, speechwriter and campaign worker for several Republican candidates in the 1950s, Herbert's knowledge of the political field was intense and intimate. His reporting style was exacting. Tim O'Reilly's exhaustive biography of Herbert made this clear: 'Herbert's pursuit of verisimilitude is extreme even for a reporter. He does not like to write about anything that he has not experienced firsthand, at least in microcosm' (1981: 13). But Herbert also had instincts for what O'Reilly would call his 'ingenious hunger for experience' when he applied for the job of Governor of American Samoa (ibid.). With the benefit of hindsight, this ambition could be considerd part of Herbert's fascination with the political impulse that led to *Dune*: 'It began with a concept: to do a long novel about the messianic convulsions which periodically inflict themselves on human societies. I had this idea that superheroes were disastrous for humans' (1981: 38).

But *Dune* also has other, more prosaic, origin points. In an interview with *Vertex Magazine*, Herbert laid out quite simply that he had too much research material *not* to produce a novel after performing some months of research for the US Department of Agriculture into sand dunes in Oregon: 'The U.S. pioneered in the control of sand dunes by planting specially developed grasses and other plants to hold a dune in the wind. You see, a sand dune is just a kind of fluid, only it takes longer for it to move' (Turner 1973: 34). The project began Herbert on a life-long interest in ecology.[3] Herbert's wife Beverly Ann Stuart was the breadwinner during this time, working as an advertising copywriter for different outlets and stores, while he assembled research for what would become *Dune*. As he researched, Herbert became both fascinated with and horrified by what humanity was doing to the planet. Ecological science fiction is often traced back to *Dune* somewhat over-enthusiastically, but it's certainly true that it presented scarcity; the regimented life-cycle of the Fremen inhabitants of Arrakis is an open comment on our own habits that appeared very early in the curve of ecology fiction (Slonczewski and Michael 2003: 183).

Dune officially began in the monthly science fiction magazine *Analog*, the first part appearing from December 1963 through to February 1964 as *Dune World*. The second part would appear from January 1965 until May that year as *The Prophet of Dune*. A great deal of mythologising has occurred around the difficulties Herbert had in pursuing book publishers; but for backgrounding the Lynch film, what's crucial is that these earlier serials have a context all their own. *Analog* was edited by the legendary John W. Campbell, whose stewardship of published American science fiction in the early 1930s was total. He worked thoroughly and intelligently with writers to expand into new genres and tropes with constant prompts. But he also developed far-right views and contrarian attitudes on slavery and civil rights, and heavily promoted pseudo-science such as Dianetics. Herbert was a 60s libertarian, a former Republican, and an independent political mind, so would have had little problem with the magazine's reputation.

The other important element of *Dune*'s initial publication is that *Analog* printed *Dune World* and *Prophet of Dune* with fresh, modern illustrations by John Schoenherr. These inky black characters, buildings and settings were drawn in obtuse compositions but perfectly clear, detailed silhouettes. Schoenherr's work is synonymous with Herbert's – these are more than likely the images that Denis Villeneuve refers to when he said that he wished to return to in order to guide a new film version. Their scale and grim grandeur added to Herbert's 'world-building'; a concept most commonly applied to science fiction and fantasy that refers to the 'creation of imaginary world and its geography, biology, cultures, etc.' that helpfully distinguishes both the creative processes and the audience relationship to science fiction (Prucher 2007: 270).

Istvan Csicsery-Ronay further delved into *Dune*'s world-building efforts and outlines the novel's use of Arabic words and language forms. His analysis is one of the most interesting passages of all scholarship on *Dune* precisely because it links the use of Arabic language to the thematic and narrative structure of the novel, faults and all. At the centre of this analysis is an important question about the language of the Fremen, which could be asked of both Herbert's *Dune* and its adaptations: 'is Arabic merely a stand-in for a wholly fictional language, used only to connote "desert culture"?' (Csicsery-Ronay 2008: 40).

Csicsery-Ronay is emphatic that these questions aren't adequately answered in *Dune* itself, and explains how this appropriation works: 'Space opera, of which *Dune* is an important example, often employs such foreign neologisms to create exotic effects. Many space operas conceal the model. Herbert's does not.' He goes on to say that, especially given the use of the term *jihad*, 'Herbert enjoyed the benefits of the ignorance and ethnocentrism of his American audience' (2008: 40). Herbert himself became fond of expanding his frame of reference as the years went on, saying in a July 1980 piece called *'Dune Genesis'* in *Omni Magazine* that 'The scarce water of *Dune* is an exact analog of oil scarcity. CHOAM is OPEC', but insisting it was just a framework for a broader critique of power (Herbert 1980: 73). Gerald Gaylard described *Dune*'s analogies in a similar way to Csicsery-Ronay: 'Herbert was not merely critiquing an abstract, mythologised imperialism', but making more concrete claims about the imperialist politicking he saw taking place at the time – even as it 'relies on audience ignorance to disguise its science fiction orientalism' (2010: 25). While *Dune*'s outright cultural appropriation is certainly dated – the same premise from an author with Frank Herbert's background would certainly not survive the grinder of twenty-first-century cultural politics – it's also essential in providing context for Herbert's approach.

Likewise, no map of *Dune*'s influences would be complete without Lesley Blanch's book *The Sabres of Paradise* (1960), a romantic tale of an Islamic holy war against Russian aggression in the Caucasus (Collins 2017). A beautifully researched retrospective piece by Hari Kunzru describes this influence and outlines the premise along more historical terms, noting that 'Paul Atreides is a young white man who fulfils a persistent colonial fantasy, that of becoming a God-king to a tribal people' (Kunzru 2015). More obviously, David Lean's *Lawrence of Arabia* (1962) and the biography of T.E. Lawrence more generally looms large in the pre-history of Herbert's novel.

The planning of attacks in both Lawrence of Arabia *and* Dune

This 'persistent colonial fantasy' about the hero and the landscape into which he enters, is a sharper critique of *Dune*, and one that foregrounds where the film expands more explicitly. Kunzru's point is that it's really the sand – not just the spice – that holds the power: 'Paul knows that if the desert planet is made to bloom, it will support a larger population, and the ethic of individualism will be eroded' (Kunzru 2015). This quasi-libertarian mythic bootstrapping strain is there in *Dune* itself: 'God created Arrakis to train the faithful' (Herbert 2010: 328). The novel's ending (and the subsequent novels) deal with the paradox of a living agent of collective will. So while the language and the entire concept of the Fremen are highly appropriative, it's more true to say that Herbert appropriated the Bedouin and their language *specifically* to furnish his universe than to say he built the universe to allegorise the Bedouin. *Dune*'s colonial premise has also been analysed in terms of President John F. Kennedy's push to transpose the irrigation and electrification projects that were transforming America to the world stage – a critical but less-discussed element of the growing sense of change in the 1960s (Hoberek 2012: 88).

Damien Broderick outlines *Dune*'s position in 1960s science fiction by describing just how fraught the landscape had become. A new wave of British authors was challenging the status quo in America, and the stale nature of repeating tropes was causing writers like Alfred Bester to demand better themes and more complex drama (Broderick 2003: 52). For Broderick, *Dune* 'manipulated superbly the longing that Bester had mocked so ferociously: an adolescent craving for imaginary worlds in which heroes triumph by a preternatural blend of bravery, genius and psi' (2003: 52). The manipulation was that *Dune* would both exalt the careening hero but ultimately reveal the terrible consequence of their centrality; power, death and fascism. Broderick goes on to say that *Dune* represented a kind of apotheosis of that Golden Age of science fiction, finally turning in on itself. The adolescent predilections for detail and power fantasies were there, but so was the dark ironic outcome (2003: 52). This was a novel about a boy playing God and finding out the limits of the fantasy, released in the same year that a *Time* magazine front cover would famously ask if 'God is dead', and a year before John Lennon announced that The Beatles were more popular that Jesus.

In the introduction to his 1985 short story collection *Eye*, Herbert gives perhaps the clearest introduction to the entire *Dune* universe – nearly thirty years after his first stories were written – reflecting on both the successes and failures of the Lynch adaptation. These quick and casual six pages are a revelation. Here he documents the constant need for bribery of Mexican officials on and around the set, a list of what he considers to be the most important scenes to be cut from the final print, his happy relationship with both Raffaella De Laurentiis and Lynch, and so on (1985: 10-11). But Herbert's biggest complaint with the film was about Paul Atreides: 'We often get non-creative leaders, people most interested in preserving their own position. They flock around centres of power.' He continues, 'Eventually, as all life does, you must encounter something you did not anticipate, and if you have not strengthened your creative resources, you will have no new ways of adapting to change' (1985: 13). Herbert is remorseless following this passage; while he's talking about Paul in the novel and film, he is also referring to Lynch, the producers at the studio, the *Dune* audiences, himself, and the political landscape of America. Referring to Jonestown, Kennedy, the Vietnam War and Hitler, Herbert crucially notes that 'mistakes made by a leader (or in a leader's name) are amplified by the numbers who follow without question' (1985: 12-13).

Herbert is crystal clear in this introduction that while bittersweet, he walked away from the Lynch film experience completely vindicated that these same sentiments that drove him to write *Dune* in the first place were well founded. Herbert's insistence that the book's central premise was not just about the ecology of the planet in a broad sense but leaders, boys, men and power aligns with a key aspect of Lynch's later oeuvre, which features men who find themselves living on top of broiling nightmares and pitted against older, more vicious men such as in *Blue Velvet*, *Twin Peaks* and *Lost Highway* (1997). Herbert ends this introduction by virtually saying goodbye to this phase of his working life:

> You and I have a compact, and my responsibility is to entertain you as richly as possible, always giving you as much extra as I can. I assume you are intelligent and will enlist your own imagination. (Herbert 1985: 14)

Herbert's defence of the film (despite admitting to concerns about its structure) is a sentiment echoed by two other crucial and contemporaneous sources; the official tie-in *The Making of Dune* (1984) by Ed Naha, a strangely comprehensive stocktake of the production process which will be drawn upon in the coming chapters, and Harlon Ellison's two-part essay in the *Magazine of Fantasy and Science-Fiction* in the American summer of 1985. Ellison, a highly prolific writer of science fiction for over fifty years, was equally known for controversies, lawsuits and various physical altercations. He was regularly asked to comment on science fiction more generally, specifically on *Dune* many times since this two-part essay. Ellison here expounded on a not-entirely-fantastic conspiracy theory, that the central problem for *Dune* as a commercial prospect was marketing – how to develop an audience for something which had no precedent, a film which appealed to the book's fans, but did not turn on its reputation in a clear and recognisable way. He argued that a schism emerged within Universal Pictures by which it became more attractive for the film to be seen as a failure; symbolic of the old studio leadership. Ellison expands on the missing material from the final cut which he felt would have made the film more narratively rich, and provides a list of scenes and presents a case for their return (Ellison 1985). These commentaries by Herbert and Ellison, both extremely influential in the science fiction literary community, set in motion a narrative that the film was gorgeous, but incomplete – that if the world couldn't have *Dune* as a Hollywood blockbuster franchise series, then the film would have to represent frustrated ambition instead, and we'd be encouraged to come back for more in another way.

Kyle MacLachlan and Frank Herbert on set (credit: Everett Collection Inc./Alamy Stock Photo)

The movie business itself would be to blame, like some amorphous beast lurking in the wild looking for anything that disturbs its peace, or attempts to eke out a life without its permission. With Herbert's phrasing 'you'll just have to wait for the mini-series' in *Eye*, and Ellison's outline of the cut material, the impetus for the Alan Smithee version was there almost immediately, and the film had its first public and apocryphal funeral; *Dune* had failed because of insufficient deference to the book, the Hollywood machine overly keen to turn it into a mass-audience event film like *Star Wars*. The worms had begun to turn.

THE SHADOW OF *STAR WARS*

There's so many ways to retrospectively analyse what *Star Wars* did for cinema; just the material changes in visual effect production alone have marked it as one of the most important points in film history (Turnock 2014). Perhaps the overwhelming vastness of its success and its 40-year domination of the genre in every conceivable commercial and social metric blinds us to different ways of thinking about what occurred around the edges of the genre during the 1980s. It certainly obscures a critical privileging of anything else in the 'space opera' subgenre or even any other interstellar science fiction films before and since.

But to think of *Star Wars* and how it contrasts with *Dune*, we can begin with tone. *Star Wars* is, amongst other things, sparkling with light physical comedy and banter. Philip Strick explains that after the first film was released, De Laurentiis was quickly 'recognising that *Dune* would have to be a deliberate counterpoint to the exuberance of *Star Wars*' (2001: 20–22). Lynch, who would turn down the opportunity to direct *Return of the Jedi* (Richard Marquand, 1983), was motivated by a similar need to strike out into the shadows. *Dune* isn't just sombre, it's *serious*. The few moments of levity are with the brutal Harkonnen characters, who spend their time sweating, suppurating and spitting through implied incest and cruel murders – quite a contrast to a smirking space smuggler looking for a quick seventeen thousand credits transporting an old man and his snotty kid companion. As Daniel Synder put it, '*Dune* was like the anti-*Star Wars*, undoing everything Lucas's trilogy did to make sci-fi a friendly place' (2014). This is, perhaps, just the start of a working comparison. In retrospect, *Dune*'s production informed it as a classical Hollywood epic, but throughout *Star Wars*, the banter and the nods to large-scale epic films already go hand in hand. The epic had already been transformed, turned into something else – partially by special effects, but, importantly, also by knowing winks and the reflexivity of the dialogue.

As for effects sequences, *Dune*'s frugality hurt but did not entirely empty the film of unique charm. While the worm-riding final battle is hardly the Death Star trench run in *Star Wars*, and the fight between Paul and Feyd is not exactly equal to the first battle between Darth Vader and Luke Skywalker in *The Empire Strikes Back* (Irvin Kershner, 1980), they both have a weird, muscular energy of their own. Similarly, the Guild Navigator 'folding space' sequence in *Dune*, with hand-animated waves of energy, lacks the brash blast of the hyperspace sequence in *Star Wars*, but adds an ichorous, mucal frenzy to faster-than-light travel. *Dune* had the reputation and expectation to exceed *Star Wars* by being smarter, grander, older – but with these effects, the universe was diminished ever so slightly. *Dune*'s universe lent itself not to the pure thrilling what-if of futurism, but of obtuse realism. Wild new technologies were made mundane by the weight of the drama above them and the mysticism involved. But as different as all involved wanted *Dune* to be from *Star Wars* – with its splash of baroque Venetian architecture, gruesome creatures, and sexual and sadistic antagonists – the former struggled with comparisons to the latter as critics and audiences finally came to see it. Herbert reflected specifically on this just a year after release, saying that they 'found sixteen points of identity between my novel and *Star Wars*' (Herbert 1985: 13).

What were these 'sixteen points of identity'? Different sources provide clashing accounts, and, to this day, it remains a popular nit-picking exercise. YouTube channels specialising in sci-fi lore have dozens of 'What *Star Wars* stole from *Dune*' variants. A boy in a desert with access to a powerful force? Princess Alia and Princess Leia? The wedge-shaped Carryall ship in *Dune* and the wedge-shaped Sandcrawler in *Star Wars*? They're certainly more than coincidences, but Lucas has rightly withstood any serious accusations over the years because *Star Wars* is, above all, a true melange.

Herbert was convinced that *Dune* had been essentially ripped off immediately after the first *Star Wars* film's release in 1977, long before Lynch came along to confer and confirm Herbert's suspicions. In a short 1977 interview called 'Should Sci-Fi Author Sue?', Herbert appeared to be considering a lawsuit:

If they (the producers of '*Star Wars*') had come to me beforehand and said, 'Hey we want to use the stuff,' I would have sent them to my agent and we would have had a very amicable agreement. (Crafts 1977)

This tells us something about both the impact *Star Wars* was having on the creative world, and what the creative impetus behind *Dune* as a movie would become over time. In the same interview, Herbert is clearly upset about *Star Wars*' success well beyond its perceived encroachment on *Dune*, saying that it 'isn't really science fiction' but 'good clean fun' and 'a comic book for the screen' (ibid.).

Star Wars being dismissed by one of literary science fiction's luminaries is no surprise, but it puts the rush to film *Dune* into context. This interview, occurring just five weeks after *Star Wars*' release, is obviously key in Herbert's reaction. He is raw, almost deflated and angry. But in these key years, *Dune*'s success was growing too. By the time he is interviewed in 1981, Herbert is buoyant and witty about *Star Wars*, talking about the changing literary landscape and his fast-growing legion of fans hungry for new epic interstellar science fiction. (Rovner 1981) And as is notable from the introduction to *Eye*, once on the other side of the Lynch production, he feels vindicated by both the Lynch film and *Star Wars* itself. Some things cinema is ready for; some things the mass audiences of cinema can accept. But perhaps not everything.

BETWEEN *STAR WARS* AND *DUNE* 1977–1984

The years between *Star Wars* and *Dune* were explosive for science fiction cinema. If Herbert and Lynch were having trouble when they set out on the project, other films similarly found trouble elsewhere in Hollywood. In *Starlog* magazine, *The Last Starfighter* (1984) director Nick Castle noted that they were running into Lucas and Spielberg 'at every turn' during the creative process, ideas already second-hand before they could be hatched (Lowry 1984). The environment around science fiction film, as we will see in the next section, was aesthetically rich and diverse. The boom in special effects production and huge appetites for high-concept sci-fi was driving up budgets and production scale. But it was *Star Wars* that was causing these movements.

Yet if we look back, the biggest problem is defining and understanding the centrality of special effects. In 1999, Brooks Landon attempted to close the loop of science fiction scholarship's big anxiety – just what *are* special effects? Landon starts with a proposition: 'Rethinking science fiction film from a perspective that centres on its special effects suggests that they function in a number of ways not necessarily subordinated to advancing narratives' (1999: 37). Then quickly, a proposition: 'special effects events can be considered self-reflexible celebrations of film technology itself' (1999: 38). That is, a looking-inward that is part of the entertainment premise of the film, part of the pleasure.

In a similar vein, Julie A. Turnock's book on this era of special effect production, *Plastic Reality*, concentrates on readdressing this period of film history – saying that the new effects culture was an 'elaboration' of the auteur ethos rather than its antithesis (2014: 2). Turnock outlines this era as an 'expanded blockbuster', taking inspiration but also formal recognition of total syntax shifts from Gene Youngblood's 1970 book *Expanded Cinema*, which linked technologies, genres and art practices in a kind of McLuhan-era manifesto for new artforms. Her 'expanded blockbuster' is an interstitial phase between the early blockbusters and what we can potentially call the post-*Terminator 2* (James Cameron, 1991) era of ubiquitous realistic effects production. In this middle phase, effects rapidly alter audience expectations; *Star Wars* accelerates a visual arms race that continues to this day. Turnock's point is that 'Rather than dismissing films and film-makers of this era for putting style before substance, it is more productive to recognize the substance of the style' (2014: 2). Interestingly, many directors took this moment to move away from 'talky scripts and literary themes', that is, to move away from projects like *Dune* (Turnock 2014: 3).

I return to Tunock's expanded blockbuster later, but this phase of science fiction films and their effects is crucial to mapping the environment that Dune landed in. By the time the American spring of 1982 arrived, *Tron* (Steven Lisberger, 1982), *Blade Runner* (Ridley Scott, 1982), *Star Trek III: The Wrath of Khan* (Nicholas Meyer, 1982) and *E.T. The Extra-Terrestrial* (Steven Spielberg, 1982) were all generating blockbuster buzz, and if *Star Wars* had cast a shadow in 1977, it was now lengthened by multiple science fiction blockbusters. Silly ones, family-friendly ones, thoughtful ones – all had found audiences (of varying sizes).

By this point, those audiences had expectations about science fiction films; more realistic special effects, new planets, props and phenomena to experience. Beyond *Star Wars*, a handful of these films are important to keep in mind alongside *Dune* for several reasons: they outline just how different the film looked, sounded and behaved and give us an impression of just how rapidly science fiction culture was changing and multiplying. By 1984, the landscape was entirely different for special effects, film narratives, budgets and audience expectations than it had been when Jodorowsky began pre-production on the first major attempt to adapt Herbert's novel. *Dune* was running out of time.

Footnotes

1. 'Alan Smithee' is a pseudonym used by directors belonging to the Director's Guild of America when they want to publicly declare their loss of creative control over a film project – through which we can confirm that David Lynch had no involvement with the re-cutting of material (Braddock and Hock 2001: 8).
2. Interestingly, Herbert himself was teaching a course simply called 'On Utopias' at the University of Washington in the years leading up to 1973, as *Dune*'s success was accelerating – what he called 'an examination of the myth of the better life' (Turner 1973: 36).
3. In a turnaround that would have amused Herbert and appealed to his sense of historical change, the very dunes that he was studying were the subject of a new US Department of Agriculture study in 2014 – how to remove the invasive species planted in the dunes by the first study (Sapp 2014).

2. THE WEIRDING WAY: THE MAKERS OF *DUNE*

> Surveying the dust-stained scene, Lynch offers a sheepish grin. 'Around here,' he laughs, '"Dune" is a four-letter word.' (Naha 1984: 10)

Film production histories perhaps naturally distill down to the core figures who made the film happen financially and creatively. In *Dune*'s case, the 'triumvirate' of the finished film is unquestionably Dino De Laurentiis, Raffaella De Laurentiis and David Lynch. Their tale is told most completely in Naha's *The Making of Dune*, an effervescent and detailed work of reportage. The book was meant as tie-in merchandise, but exceeds that category by outlining the difficulties and contradictions in production through extensive interviews with the cast and crew. While this chapter will refer to Naha extensively, it is important to contextualise it: it also bears the hallmarks of what was, as Princess Irulan (played by Virginia Madsen) would have it, 'a very delicate time'. Through the screenplay development period, *Dune* changed a great deal – a common fate for a project worth tens of millions of dollars. Less commonly, *Dune* changed dramatically between principal photography and release, and it also changed Lynch himself. The stories told about *Dune*'s production have themselves changed over time to suit new contexts and fit new narratives. Part of this story is explicit: to become the quirky-yet-intellectual art-house darling 'David Lynch', that person needed to be seen in opposition to and an escapee from the Hollywood machine, and *Dune* needed to be rejected, a failure. But that wasn't always the case.

Throughout all the interviews, tell-alls, feature pieces and previews leading up to the film's release, it is clear that *Dune* was a massive and difficult production, but not 'troubled' in the euphemistic language used to mean continuous clashes and fights on set or production fund shortfalls. Or, more precisely, not those things to the exclusion of all else. A picture emerges of a film produced exactly as the main powerbrokers wanted it made, edited to produce a commercially viable object, and finally released in a wash of relief, confusion and delight. In fact, several key cast and crew recount the filming of *Dune* as an overwhelmingly well-organised and creatively fulfilling experience – stories increasingly obscured by the simpler but untrue story that the film was always somehow 'destined' to fail. If *Jodorowsky's Dune* told a tale of a manic, high-pitched unmade film emanating from a great mind to bear witness to an equally great moment in counter-culture, then what on earth was Lynch's *Dune*? Is it a paean to pre-computer generated special effects – the last attempt to produce science fiction in the old mould of cerebral weirdness? Is it an art-house director's failed attempt to tame the worst instincts of the Hollywood machine – giving up the right to a final cut in a misguided compromise? Did it represent a collective desire for dense and mysterious science fiction in the shadow of the great massification over at Lucasfilm?

This chapter will delve into the details of *Dune*'s production, but also plant some flags in the desert and place it within both the David Lynch and science fiction canons. First, I compare the artistic visions of Jodorowsky, Ridley Scott and Lynch – each attached to the project at different stages – as they orbited the possibility of making *Dune*. Second, I outline the events of the energetic phase that brought the project to fruition; as Raffaella and Dino De Laurentiis folded time and space to make it happen. Third, I delve into the Lynch cosmos to map some of the connections between *Dune* and his work before and since, staking out a claim that *Dune* can no more be rejected from his oeuvre than any other film, regardless of the determination of critics, and his own repeated insistence. Finally, I sketch out the significant relationships and individuals during filming and pre-production as I identify the main cast and crew of *Dune*.

HOUSE JODOROWSKY AND HOUSE SCOTT

Before the more famous Jodorowsky, Scott and Lynch stewardships of the film adaptation of *Dune*, Herbert sold an option to Arthur P. Jacobs, the producer who had handled *Planet of the Apes* (Franklin J. Schaffner, 1968) and its sequels. While Jacobs' attempt to bring *Dune* to the screen had its own dramas – including the very brief involvement of the acclaimed David Lean, director of *Lawrence of Arabia* and *Doctor Zhivago* (1965) – it was cut short by the producer's death at the age of 51. Herbert would later comment dryly that 'he didn't consult me on that, either' (Lewis 1985: 8). Lean's extraordinary talents would have combined with long-term script collaborator

Robert Bolt, who had worked on both *Lawrence* and *Zhivago* and won an Oscar for the latter, but yet another story treatment was produced by the time Jacobs died.

Released in 2013, Frank Pavich's extraordinary documentary *Jodorowsky's Dune* breathlessly tells the story of the Chilean visionary's attempt from 1973 to 1975 to pull together *Dune* as a Technicolor extravaganza. It was to star Mick Jagger, Salvador Dali, Orson Wells, Gloria Swanson and Jodorowsky's own son as Paul, and would be built from a near-legendary compendium of sketches, storyboards and design work by a team of artists and craftspeople including Rene 'Moebius' Girard, Dan O'Bannon, Ron Cobb and H.R. Giger. As Jodorowsky tells it, the unmade film promised to be a culmination of not only the novel's core languages, but a whole new science fiction film language. The documentary claims – not entirely without merit – that the pre-production of the film subsequently fed significant creative ideas into the worlds of *Alien* (Ridley Scott, 1979), *Star Wars*, *The Terminator* (James Cameron, 1984), and much contemporary science fiction cinema.

Jodorowsky's Dune is an irresistible tale, full of passion and drama. By showing that *Star Wars* (as well as *Alien*) both benefited from the minor but notable cultural hype in science fiction magazines and culture built up around Jodorowsky's project, what seems like an accident of zeitgeist and timing is given real, concrete form. One of the ways the documentary told this tale was by celebrating the rich body of actual pre-production materials built up by the team. When it does return to the question of timing, it then does so with authority, telling a story science fiction fans can intuit to be 'true' by what they already know. As Peter Debruge puts it, 'even in its still-born form, the film manifested the sort of collective conscious that Jodorowsky was trying to peddle through its plot, trickling down to influence other sci-fi films that followed' (2013).

This idea of the 'collective conscious' (practically interchangeable here with the Jung-era concept of 'collective unconscious') should be anathema to our interest in historical detail; tropes, genres and creative histories are made up of material and 'real' things, and ideas can be mapped even if documentation is scarce. This is what makes *Jodorowsky's Dune* and its focus on the artists so revelatory – it is something to hold on to, our map in an amorphous space. This image begat that image, this idea begat that idea. Yet we can't ignore the idea of mystical purpose and timing entirely. David Lynch explicitly believes in it and makes films about it. Alejandro Jodorowsky explicitly believes in it and makes films about it. Frank Herbert explicitly believed it and wrote books about it. All three were, at various points, informed or invested in making art, writing, and thinking about manifesting unconscious thoughts and desires, and what it means. The *Star Wars* and *Dune* narrative universes centre around the awakening of a collective consciousness or force. In typical Lynch fashion, he tapped into this sense of time and cultural valance in a cover note to the fifth version of his *Dune* script: 'Curiosity concerning "*Dune*" is like steam in a giant boiler. It is already building up considerable pressure. Any leaks concerning what we are doing on this project will decrease the curiosity factor and cause us to lose power.'[4]

What is startling about *Jodorowsky's Dune* is the absolute raw *material* strength of the pre-production drawing, design and production materials presented in an endless series of intoxicating montages. These materials provoke a core question: what would Jodorowsky's version actually be like? As exciting as the documentary is, as passionate as he is about a particular vision, and how obvious the impact of the pre-production work on its various participants, while enticing, the answer isn't exactly clear – it can't be, because it was never made. It therefore feels unsatisfying to hear him dismiss the Lynch version so summarily; understandable in context, but also almost cruel. Jodorowsky's vision – although different – was that of a driving, harsh, lysergic, mutant epic that would send Herbert fans running for the hills. His story of going to see the finished film with his sons reveals how much he needed Lynch's film to fail for his *own* story to be complete – for his vision to be vindicated.

Perhaps Jodorowsky's final version of *Dune* would have met with much more excitement in some respects, and produced something catastrophically and magically different. While watching the documentary, or the earlier *Moebius Redux: A Life in Pictures* (Hasko Baumann, 2007), it is clear the major players all have a deep cultural intelligence and profound hands-on knowledge of what images can do. What makes the anecdotes about Jodorowsky's attempt to make *Dune* so compelling is how they reveal the inner workings of a vast subterranean creative system in its exploded diagram of frustrated ambition.

Alejandro Jodorowsky interviewed in Jodorowsky's Dune *(Frank Pavich, 2013)*

From the perspective of Lynch's *Dune*, Pavich's documentary was on its release celebrated for its emphatic energy which led many pop culture websites in the months after its release back to Lynch's version in a number of retrospective articles. Perhaps more tellingly, it is directly after *Jodorowsky's Dune* release that fan-run YouTube channels began to produce videos reflecting on both the made and unmade versions of *Dune*. YouTube's 'vernacular creativity' culture means that the value of videos is their ability to help you form and grow social networks (Burgess and Green 2013: 26), but there's another facet of this popularity: the resurfacing and re-uploading of rare interviews, rare quotes, and forgotten materials for people to resurrect in the new light garnered through the documentary's popularity.

Although some speculated after the release of *Jodorowsky's Dune* about how computer-generated imagery may today give Jodorowsky license to produce a remarkable version, it's the quality of the development work by the group – especially the artwork by Jean Girard – that should be privileged here as much as Jodorowsky himself. This work, after all, was actually created, we have more than vague gesticulations towards its possible potential. This aspect of pre-production practice transformed the working lives of several of the most important illustrators and concept artists of the twentieth century, but more than that, artists such as Girard were mutating the deeply planned, deeply interconnected and deeply loved

Dune universe and treating it not as an act of translation, or of some loosely defined taste-driven inspiration, but something new. The Jodorowsky group was using *Dune* – with all its intricacies – like a calculator or computer; where ideas could be turned into something else, something fungible. This ultimately failed to attract enough production funding to go ahead, but had begun to plant seeds of anticipation in both film production circles, and even the public, as fragments of the project leaked.

Ridley Scott's interest in *Dune* is less well-known than Jodorowsky's, and certainly did not progress as far, but is regardless still interesting for several reasons. Dino De Laurentiis bought the rights from the French consortium that had attached Jodorowsky, and in 1978 returned to Herbert for a new script. A year later, De Laurentiis hired Scott for the project, and screenwriter Rudy Wurlitzer – who wrote screenplays for films including *Two-Lane Blacktop* (Monte Hellman, 1971) and *Pat Garrett and Billy the Kid* (Sam Peckinpah, 1973) – to produce a new script. Sources vary wildly in their versions of events, but Scott's success with *Alien* and the changing landscape of science fiction cinema were clearly in De Laurentiis's mind. Wurlitzer's script apparently focused on the incestuous relationship between Paul and his mother in the novel, and Scott wanted to split the story into two films' worth at some point. Both the Herbert book series and Lynch's version play with incestuous elements, but this version would have developed it further: Paul would surely therefore have become as taboo as the xenomorph in *Alien*.[5] Scott would drop out for a combination of reasons; chief among them the untimely death of his brother Frank in 1980.

With Herbert still smarting from the success of *Star Wars* at the end of 1977, and the move from Jodorowsky to De Laurentiis / Scott in 1978 and 1979, this period must have been an anxious one for all involved. Herbert voiced frustration with Jodorowsky's attempt, complaining that 'it was the size of a phonebook, and pretty anti-Catholic too' (Naha 1984: 15). Of Scott's attempt, Herbert was merely bemused by the incest-heavy script but felt the possibilities of a movie actually being made were diminishing. Yet both De Laurentiis senior and junior were determined to find a working production model; for Dino, '*Dune* was the kind of movie that I wanted to have a strong hand in … I had to be able to call the shots' (Naha 1984: 15).

HOUSE DE LAURENTIIS

While Dino De Laurentiis is often credited as the progenitor of the film's final form – not without good reason – it's in retrospect we can see the huge impact of his daughter Raffaella throughout the pre-production phase. Dino had slowly moved his focus to America after decades of working in Italian film production, gathering a reputation as a risk-taker and an important figure in Italian neo-realism; Vittorio De Sica, Roberto Rossellini, Luchino Visconti and Federico Fellini all made films with De Laurentiis's help, and Fellini's *La Strada* (1954) and *Le Notti di Cabiria* (1956) both won Oscars for Best Foreign Language Film.

Across his lengthy career, Dino built an appetite for large-scale, complex epics such as *Ulysses* (Mario Camerini, 1954), *War and Peace* (King Vidor, 1956) and *The Bible ... In the Beginning* (John Huston, 1966). At one point, he considered this last film suitable for a 15-hour version with multiple directors and special screening arrangements before reality rudely intervened. But while these are considered his true epics, two others are worthy of special mention. Richard Fleischer's *Barabbas* (1961) was a sprawling Biblical epic featuring a crucifixion scene filmed during the total solar eclipse visible over Italy in 1961. Huge sets and astonishing numbers of extras parade around the screen with much pomp and circumstance. The trailer for *Barabbas* would dramatically intone that 'soon you will experience a motion picture of unparalleled inspiration and unparalleled magnificence'; perhaps a foreshadowing of the *Dune* poster's tagline, 'A place beyond your dreams. A movie beyond your imagination.' Likewise, Sergei Bondarchuk's *Waterloo* (1970) was a visually spectacular recreation of the battle of the same name, starring Rod Steiger, Christopher Plummer and Orson Welles, as King Louis XVIII. The film is famous for using 15,000 soldiers from the Soviet army arranged by Soviet film company Mosfilm, as well as 2,000 trained cavalrymen. A complex system of translators working over walkie-talkies, a permanent army camp, and helicopter camera systems were all employed to make this film happen.[6]

Dino's love of large scale film production was passed to his children. De Laurentiis's years of marriage to iconic Italian actor Silvana Mangano produced four children, all of whom became involved in film to various degrees. Most involved in the family business was Raffaella, whose journey through art school provided her with a guided intuition for organisation and production. In the years leading up to *Dune*, she had worked in Tahiti not only to produce films, but to oversee construction of a hotel to house their crews during production. One day she would leave a note on her father's desk that read 'No matter what happens during the time I'm away, you're not allowed to start *Dune* without me!' (Naha 1984: 17)

Raffaella was instrumental in gathering the professional forces and turning her father's attention towards the project. She had wrapped production on the first *Conan* film (John Milius, 1982) during *Dune*'s Ridley Scott phase, and the timing and her own ambitions meant she was given the lead in finding a way forward for *Dune*. Enter David Lynch: Raffaella's years of work in the business had made her unsentimental about cinema, but she confessed to crying for the first time in years after seeing Lynch's *The Elephant Man* (Naha 1984: 18). Lynch had not read *Dune* when he was first approached, and when responding to a phone call proposing the project, he kept asking 'June? June?'. He also had doubts about working with the De Laurentiis family, saying Dino had a reputation for 'movie-mogul stuff' (Naha 1984: 22). Initial meetings erased these doubts, as Lynch found Dino to be warm, friendly, unrushed and creative. Lynch recalls their second meeting in which Dino talked about everybody's favourite animals as a kind of jovial group bonding strategy.

David Lynch and Raffaella De Laurentiis on set (credit: Everett Collection Inc./Alamy Stock Photo)

Lynch's image has always been that of a quiet, unassuming lad from Missoula, Montana, existing on the fringes of the Hollywood production system. But in the accounts of the genesis of *Dune*, Lynch is marked as a professional armed with the knowledge, connections and instinct to weigh up the hefty decisions required for a major movie of this scale. Before his doubts about the screenplay development process, Lynch saw great potential in a book he hadn't even finished reading, and shared a genuine passion for film that the De Laurentiis family embodied.

Once script development had begun in earnest, Dino invited Lynch to come to Venice. Dino, exhausted from a series of mud baths, took Raffaella and David from the town of Aveno for a gondola ride into Venice. Dino alighted the group at a certain location, and walked a specific route to take them into Saint Mark's Square (Piazza San Marco) 'in the most perfect way' (Godwin 2016: 276). Dino and Raffaella were clearly turning on the charm, and at the same time, Lynch was exposed to one of the most unique and beautifully-constructed environments in the world. Dino bought Lynch a tourist book of photos of the square, visited a favourite cappuccino haunt, and they had an 'incredible' meal on the island of Torcello nearby (ibid.). The impact on Lynch's creative inspiration for *Dune* was immediate, wild and powerful. He credits that day with the impetus to create the planet Caladan as a quasi-baroque state weighed down by a long-past Renaissance. In turn, seeing dark buildings that same night that seemed to have no clear entrance or exit solved how to imagine Giedi Prime, home of the Harkonnen (Godwin 2016: 279). In an interview from October 1984, Lynch said that the trip, a book bought along the way, and the art history research they inspired, combined to spark *Dune*'s process in earnest (Mandell 1984: 48).

This event played a significant role in Lynch finding a visual language to make sense of Herbert's universe. He believed that the setting could be heavily influenced by a 'renaissance or something five thousand years ago' and that 'all the technology, everything was built, done so well and it was done so richly and it just lasted' (Godwin 2016: 279). Some of this iconography is in the novel, but at other points (such as in the scenes on Caladan), we see Venice very clearly in the film's curious ossified ornamentalism. The legend is complete: Dino, fresh from his mud baths, beckoning through an entryway. The ambitious young director follows through. The glory of the red Campanile tower. The ideas tick over. Thoughts acquire speed.

In Kenneth George Godwin's on-set diary, Raffaella is clearly the dominant family member day-to-day on the production, with Dino making an appearance here and there. Godwin's diary, first published in 1983 and updated in 2015 and 2016 with previously unreleased transcripts of un-aired interviews, is a remarkable document on a number of fronts. It was generated through months of continuous access to the set, with a view that Godwin and cameraman Anatol Pacanowski would help produce a making-of featurette. That never eventuated, and the diary emerges with extremely raw and no-doubt unpleasant revelations from Universal Pictures' point of view. It contains scans of call sheets, descriptions of arguments, budget cuts, chaotic stunt filming and hellish anecdotes about high drama and drunken actors. Most revealing isn't the chaos of production, however, but its relative calm given the conditions, the number of publicists, and the broad inherent strangeness in the approach to the material. Raffaella cuts a sympathetic figure, even as Godwin's account puts her at the centre of unpleasantness and disorganisation towards the end of production.

Raffaella was also producing *Conan The Destroyer* (Richard Fleischer, 1984) as *Dune* wound down, with some of that film also shot in Mexico's Churubusco Studios. A picture emerges of a producer working within a changing system at a crucial point in film history. Genres such as science fiction and fantasy were slipping out of the grasp of studios like those of the De Laurentiis family; *Legend* (Ridley Scott, 1985), *Labyrinth* (Jim Henson, 1986) and *The Princess Bride* (Rob Reiner, 1987) tilted the fantasy film towards expressive romps and away from meticulous epics. *Dune*'s $40 million budget is evident in long shots of large crowds and expansive battle sequences in the desert. But only two years later, James Cameron's blistering *Aliens* (1986) would be made for less than half that and looked as if it cost ten times more. The *Conan* films dated quickly in some respects, but had high camp aesthetics in which to revel. *Dune*, for all its charms, did not. Suddenly, the De Laurentiis approach which had allowed the family such freedom was a liability. Godwin's account is sour: 'The cameras are out-dated Todd- AO, because De Laurentiis owns the company. This stuff was the hot new thing in the mid-Fifties, but it's long since been by-passed' (Godwin 2016: 21). Yet this doesn't explain a particular failure of production: if the De Laurentiis production method was economical, it nevertheless produced large-scale epics with thousands of extras, *Dune* included. Perhaps what Godwin was keyed into was the difference in approach; De Laurentiis was making the best use of the knowledge, material, and expertise on hand just as the new breed of special-effects blockbuster was demanding ever more shocking newness with each ticket sale. The 'expanded blockbuster' was in a very delicate period, and mistakes could be made if the public were misjudged (Turnock 2014).

Lynch's *Dune* was as much Raffaella's *Dune*, and her pride was not only in the finished film but the process taken to get there; all of the questions she would get about her youth and gender were ignored, and she promoted the film as if it was headed for greatness. During the first crucial weeks of the film's release, before the negative narrative had taken hold, Lynch and Raffaella took to the stage in England as part of *The Guardian* Lectures series during the film's press tour, interviewed by Chris Auty. Raffaella explained what she hopes the appeal of the film will be:

> I feel that I've done something new for the industry and that is something to be proud of. I think there's going to be around *Dune* in the eighties the same kind of mood and feel and controversy that was around 2001. (Raffaella de Laurentiis, quote in The Guardian Lectures 1985)

Years later, Raffaella is still a staunch defender of the finished film, yet sanguine enough about some of the decisions that were made to offer an alternative reading. An interview with Raffaella from Sanctuary's 'Special Edition' *Dune* DVD of 2004 summarises a wry commentary on the critical reception of the film with 'but those that love it, *love* it'. In the introduction to Universal's 'Extended Edition' DVD (2006), she presents her view; they had a complex book to adapt, took a lot of risks, had some production issues, and the resultant movie is difficult but beautiful. In these quotes, Raffaella is more than the producer looking back – with Dino gone and with Lynch categorically disinterested, she is still the film's torchbearer, as she was at the beginning. Her relationship with Lynch was certainly complex; in 1986, when she had her uterus removed, she knew it would make a perfect gift for Lynch, sending it to him in a sealed jar of formaldehyde (O'Mahony 2002). Their chemistry seems to have been the catalyst by which the film took its unusual course to production. One passage from a *Rolling Stone* interview illustrates this more candidly than anywhere else. At once, it illustrates their relationship, Lynch's inability to compromise, and illuminates the strange origin of *Dune*'s many dogs: 'If you're ready to shoot something, and suddenly he decides he wants twenty-eight dogs running up and down the hall, you've got to find twenty-eight dogs' (Hodenfield 1984: 26). For all the sympathies we can have with Lynch being unable to express himself inside a big-budget production, the vicissitudes of the genius auteur's sudden ideas make work difficult for many more people (and animals) who are working to a collective plan.⁷

HOUSE LYNCH

Some biographers, writers and academics whose works on Lynch often span hundreds of pages will sometimes go to great length to not discuss *Dune*. For example, Thierry Jousse's otherwise excellent Lynch entry in the *Masters of Cinema* series for *Cahiers du cinema* gives it no more than 200 words, the highlight of which is the two-sentence summary execution of the 'catastrophically awful music by the 1980s group Toto' (2010: 28). Scanning down the table of contents for Justus Nieland's otherwise thoughtful eponymous book on Lynch, the analysis of the films is divided into 'Interior Design', 'The Art of Being Moved' and 'Organism'; each then divided into four chapters connected to a key film. *Dune* is not one of the twelve representative films. Flicking to the rear of the book, the index reveals the status of Dune among this constellation; one lone entry, that refers to the film only as a 'debacle' (Nieland 2012: 28).

It's hard not to read this attitude through *Dune*'s own mythology: the poisonous water of life is consumed, the sleeper awakens, and he now knows what he has to do. Of course, Nieland's analysis is perfectly accurate – *Dune* is far more a film of collaborative outcomes than even the most loosely arranged auteur narrative can contain. For most, that was not enough. As *Dune* is inevitably compared to Lynch's major works on either side – *Eraserhead*, *The Elephant Man*, *Blue Velvet*, *Wild at Heart* (1990) and *Twin Peaks* – it becomes absolutely necessary even today to excise the aberrant object; explicitly and repeatedly.

If Nieland was unforgiving of *Dune*, Alister Mactaggart's *The Film Paintings of David Lynch: Challenging Film Theory* was utterly unapologetic. Of *Dune*, he declares: 'I could not bring myself to write about it – it drives me mad. ... It would interfere with and diminish the pleasure of the other films' (Mactaggart 2010: 162). What could be more powerful than a film that destroys and diminishes other films?

This is not merely a personal reaction or taste issue. To make sense of Lynch's directorial language, to make him an artist, to maintain academic faith in auteur theory more broadly, *Dune* has to be ignored. For some, it even has to die. It's the ugly painting in the study, proof of a different and difficult truth. This attitude should be resisted. *Dune* simply reveals too much about the vicissitudes of film-making, the compromises of production, and most crucially, it retains too many signature Lynch elements to be ignored. It doesn't fit the artist-sanctioned ideal, the authorial brand, to the point where the most academic positions sometimes avert their gaze to avoid the re-evaluation it would require.

This *Dune*-blindness within Lynch discourse extends beyond film academia. David Foster Wallace's famous 1996 essay about Lynch describes *Dune* as 'unquestionably the worst movie of Lynch's career', and Wallace goes in for one of his all-time great killing blows as he describes the film as 'the kind of debacle that in myths about Innocent, Idealistic Artists in the Maw of the Hollywood Process signals the violent end of the artist's Innocence' (Foster Wallace: 1996). Wallace's burial of the film is – because myth-making is so often done literally – even in a section called 'A Quick Sketch of Lynch's Genesis as a Heroic Auteur'.

Anthony Todd's *Authorship and the Films of David Lynch* (2012) comes at *Dune*'s placement in the authorial system as a fixed reading problem. He explores why people insist on either calling *Dune* a Lynch film, or why they don't, and is heavily oriented towards a Roland Barthes/Michel Foucault-infused reading of the author as a modernist construct. Seeing auteurism through an ideological lens, Todd offers a wry thought experiment in which 'we might discard any Lynchian readings of *Dune* as little more than hermeneutic wish fulfilment and claim that any salient authorship is imagined rather than actual' (2012: 56). While acknowledging the shortcomings of this approach, Todd nevertheless forecloses on the film as a commercial object and says that 'those who subscribe to the wisdom of authorial or auteurist essentialism will do so in defiance of logic' (2012: 60). It's a wild turnaround to insist that Lynch, of all directors, should be assessed with logic – but even accepting Todd's dismissal that a book like this one represents 'hermeneutic wish fulfilment', I can only respond that we should be less interested in a 'Lynchian reading of *Dune*' than a *Dune*-ian reading of Lynch. The latter here is in part what this book seeks to provide.

In her book *The Passion of David Lynch*, Martha Nochimson says it best: *Dune* is 'the only Lynch film about which there is a valid general agreement that it doesn't work' (1997: 127). Yet, its 'beautiful, inventive images' resurface in 'later work to become the foundation of effective storytelling' (ibid.). If effective storytelling often really just means effective film-making *per se*, then Nochimson's appraisal of the film balances the various viewpoints that situate the film either outside the Lynch canon, an object lesson in Hollywood excess, or out of date futurism.

Erica Sheen's nuance is that while people want to call Lynch an auteur, his 'working practices articulate the complexities of a system' that doesn't think of directors and auteurs in the same way (Sheen 2004: 40). Sheen's work is notable for a diversion to analyse why the auteur approaches explain but can never analyse *Dune*. To do so, she extensively covers a Sci-Fi Channel online discussion panel that was timed to coincide with the screening of the 2000 miniseries *Frank Herbert's Dune*. They discuss the film and propose alternative versions of shots, premises and actors. Sheen ends her description by noting that their speculations represent counterfactual thinking, 'an activity rarely acknowledged in academic paradigms of spectatorship but fundamental to the way film-makers and their audiences live together inside the thinking machine of cinema' (2004: 46). In this phrase, we have something truly telling. Speculation inside the thinking machine is natural; it's part of the imaginative and participatory energy of social spectatorship. Different and future narratives and endings, different dialogues and actions. There seem to be two places in the wide field of David Lynch scholarship which seem to attract this kind of analysis; first, around *Twin Peaks* – in which we can recall Ndalianis's 'conditions, secret ingredients and magic potions that generate the cult experience' specific to serial television (Ndalianis 2011: 63); and second, if rarely, in reference to the aberrant *Dune*. Science fiction, not alone but certainly importantly amongst film genres, lends itself to this kind of viewing through our manifold eye. This is the guesswork of science fiction; mysterious objects that contain unexplained technologies, obscure character revelations reliant on stylistic largesse; complex universes rendered in broad strokes. From this perspective, *Dune* as a finished work – whoever claims or denies ownership of it – perhaps then requires *both* the science fiction eye and the Lynchian eye to see through to the film's textures.

This Lynchian eye – his vision of the world as expressed in his work – is different, but not so frighteningly complex as some of the scholarship makes it. For one, it requires only a brief sketch of his meditation practice; so often overlooked in the rush to find answers more fitting for film theory. Lynch was practicing Transcendental Meditation (TM) for nearly eleven years by the time *Dune* was released and his primary outputs on social media for the last few years have been his Festival of Disruption, promotion of the Maharishi School of Management's various courses and fairly constant activity promoting TM through donations, programs, teaching and organisations. TM is such a crucial practice for Lynch that he encourages his interlocutors, colleagues and interviewers to begin training in TM. His daily, life-encompassing ritual – 20 minutes of focussed peace, twice a day, empowered by mantras – is either ignored in Lynch discourse, or, in rare cases, focussed on to the exclusion of all else.

Yet Martha Nochimson's second book on Lynch has a strongly-worded Preface that makes an impassioned plea to change the way we talk about David Lynch – specifically to include his belief systems, with TM at the centre. She warns that 'misprisions have been caused by critics' overdependence on psychology', criticising the reliance on Lacanian thought and Freudian psychoanalysis to study his work (2014: xiii). But she also does more than this: she argues that Western thought itself is inadequate, or at best an incomplete guide to Lynch's artistic purposes. Instead, she advises to pay attention to his 'impressionistic grasp of physics', his study of Vedic traditions, and his meditation practices to produce a critical eye attuned enough to grasp what he produces. Nochimson punctuates this call with this startling declaration: 'His is a more complex modern vision than has been attempted by any other American film-maker' (2014: xv). There is complexity to unpick, and a unique cosmology, but rather than treating this as an issue of scale – the *most* different, the *most* complex – and giving Lynch a nearly omnipotent quasi-Kwisatch Haderach position in our quest for meaning, Nochimson's plea is interesting for another reason. Lynch treats matter – the very idea of matter – differently. He treats it like others treat the mind and its workings. Matter can be jealous, paranoid, happy, but it also has rules. Once you accept that notion, then Lynch's work is not more magically 'complex' or 'difficult', but in fact often brazenly, blindingly clear. A Francis Bacon painting is materially, socially and emotionally dense – but it is often also brazenly, blindingly *clear*.

Thinking more about TM and Vedic traditions will guide us towards what Lynch thinks. Nochimson argues this by pointing out that 'the task at hand' – that is, criticism – is a matter of navigating the beliefs of the artist, and the beliefs of the society which produced them (2014: xv). While that's a great working definition in some respects, it means that a film like *Dune* can only be measured by how much it isn't an artist's work to begin with: it reconfigures the film to be a failure machine. True to her ethos, Nochimson has also taken on TM herself through studying and meeting Lynch, providing her with personal as well as professional insight into his process.

We should also ask whether psychoanalytical readings and classic film studies is something a director's work just gets to step away from because they opt for something outside the orthodox norms of contemporary Western spiritual belief. I'd argue very strongly in the negative. Lynch's filmic treatment of women, of race, of sex, of power may be heavily informed by his practices, but they also need interrogating for what they say about and their place in the world that we *all* live in, regardless of our spirituality. We can be sympathetic to Nochimson's frustrations with cinema studies' tendencies to apply in a blanket manner some unyielding theory as a means of tunnelling through a text, but we don't need to engage with TM to engage with a Lynch film. What we can take from Lynch's critics into reading *Dune* makes up an entirely different alchemy – a grasp of his visual and sonic fascinations, knowledge that his creative language is informed by meditation, his use of mantras and what they mean for his direction of acting performance, and his life-long concern with responding to physical matter like a sculptor, artist or woodworker. Lynch, through his own words and reinforced by biographers and critics ad nauseum, is fascinated by film first and foremost as *matter*.

These were the elements that he brought into the crucible of making a large-scale science fiction film, alongside a powerfully driven producer and an experienced financier looking for a standout hit. Lynch's sensibility was to be their sharpest edge – their collective edge, it must be emphasised – for straddling the huge gulfs between the material and the marketplace. The film bears his mark all too well, but even his name was not his alone. The house of Lynch, as it is with any director, was a stand-in for a collective will focussed through a single eye. As I now outline, familiar and future collaborators would expand around this triumvirate as production accelerated.

THE LITTLE MAKERS: CAST AND CREW

There are a number of other key figures essential to the story of Lynch's *Dune*. Throughout 1982, Raffaella, Dino and David Lynch organised the production with a view to finding a studio complex big enough – but cheap enough – to make an epic. Raffaella's choice of Churubusco Studios in Mexico City came after an exhaustive campaign to find a complex that was near a desert but had multiple sound stages free for a long period of time (Naha 1984: 25). Lynch brought on some former collaborators early in the process. Freddie Francis joined as cinematographer, coming off work on Lynch's *The Elephant Man* and *The French Lieutenant's Woman* (Karel Reisz, 1981) and over two decades since his Oscar-winning cinematography for *Sons and Lovers* (Jack Cardiff, 1960). Frederick Elmes would join as second unit director, having been Lynch's cinematographer on *Eraserhead*. Alan Splet lead the sound design, after working with Lynch on both *The Grandmother* (1970) and *Eraserhead*.

At the beginning of the crew assembly process, production designer Tony Masters was brought on board; he had worked on *2001: A Space Odyssey* and as art director for *Lawrence of Arabia*, both films looming large in the triumvirate's artistic ambitions. Bob Ringwood of *Excalibur* (John Boorman, 1981) fame would lead costume design – his work on that underrated fantasy film raised the bar for the genre just as it seemed to be entering hibernation. Ringwood's shop for *Dune*, including experienced assistant Debbie Phipps, famously used old bodybags for the Spacing Guild suits and produced dozens of intricate hats for the Fremen that never made it to the screen.

As Masters assembled a team of illustrators and draftspeople, the De Laurentiis network would draw in Aldo Puccini as construction manager, who had worked through many of their films, from *La Strada* to *Conan the Barbarian*. Emilio Ruiz Del Rio would lead the charge on miniatures development, also having worked on Conan with the family after a long career, including work on *Dr. Zhivago* and *Solomon and Sheba* (King Vidor, 1959). Editor Antony Gibbs would go on to work on many De Laurentiis productions, no doubt having proven that if he could edit *Dune* from over three hours to just over two, he was capable of anything.

With much of the crew being drawn from Churubusco's networks and local production systems, a lot of *Dune*'s story sits within a context of Mexican production. Although very little evidence remains among the production diaries, materials and interviews, a single line in Godwin's diary indicates that context was fraught, when he notes that 'there's a lot of local resentment against the production and the secrecy surrounding it' (Godwin 2016: 35). No doubt the choice of location was disputed; Raffaella once bluntly stated 'I think the fact we all hated Mexico so badly also made us closer' (Strauss 1984: 7). There's a great deal to be read between the lines elsewhere in the material; unsourced complaints about the facilities at Churubusco slide into racist-sounding generalisations about Mexican working practices in the interviews, often in third-hand innuendo, and comments about 'the locals' – treated as if they were challenges to overcome by the *proper* working people on set.

With the complex production in full swing, finding the cast would evolve organically with Lynch drafting the help of casting director Jane Jenkins, coming off David Cronenberg's *The Dead Zone* (1983) and who would continue her successful career with cult films including *Ferris Bueller's Day Off* (John Hughes, 1986), *Beetlejuice* (Tim Burton, 1988) and *Jurassic Park* (Steven Spielberg, 1993). The Emperor Shaddam IV was played by José Ferrer, father of Miguel Ferrer who would play FBI Agent Albert Rosenfield in both *Twin Peaks*, *Twin Peaks: Fire Walk With Me* (1993), and *Twin Peaks: The Return*. Ferrer Sr. had achieved the peak of his fame in the 1940s and 1950s for multiple performances of iconic seventeenth-century French libertine Cyrano De Bergerac, culminating in a Best Actor Oscar in 1950 for his performance in Michael Gordon's film of the same name. He was the first Hispanic actor to win a major Academy Award, and his career in the intervening decades included spectacular turns in *Lawrence of Arabia* and *The Greatest Story Ever Told* (George Stevens, 1965).

Reverend Mother Gaius Helen Mohiam – introduced alongside the Emperor – is played by Sîan Phillips, whose vast accomplishments on stage, television and film peak with the role of the wise-cracking Livia in the 13-episode series *I, Cladius* (Herbert Wise, 1976). Her role is largely limited to earlier scenes, but she nevertheless leaves her mark, as her stern admonishments and barely concealed spite propel Paul Atreides out of safety. Virginia Madsen plays Princess Irulan, a role that could have expanded greatly in the abandoned sequels, as her character is central to the novel's premise and setting. Madsen's career was just starting at this point, and she would go on to have impeccable genre credentials with major roles in *Highlander II: The Quickening* (Russell Mulcahy, 1991), *Candyman* (Bernard Rose, 1992) and angel-horror cult classic *The Prophecy* (Gregory Widen, 1995), finally attaining mainstream success with an Academy Award nomination for *Sideways* (Alexander Payne, 2004).

Iconic Swedish actor Max Von Sydow plays Doctor Kynes, a 'Judge of the Change' acclimatised to Arrakis, with brimming confidence and undisturbed peace.[8] A consummate actor most famous for his key performances in a number of Ingmar Bergman films including *The Seventh Seal* (1957), he had worked on multiple Dino De Laurentiis productions in the years prior as Ming the Merciless in *Flash Gordon* and King Osric in *Conan The Barbarian*. In Godwin's interview with Von Sydow, the actor was clearly aware that his role has been cut cruelly short in *Dune*, adding wistfully that he wished it had been a television series (Godwin 2016: 318).

Playing Duke Leto Atreides is Jurgen Prochnow, already an accomplished screen actor who appeared in *The Lost Honour of Katharina Blum* (Volker Schlöndorff and Margarethe von Trotta, 1975) and *Das Boot* (Wolfgang Petersen, 1981). His accent comes up as a concern in the Naha book but adds a great deal to a crucial moment where he says he's proud of his son, Paul. Prochnow would receive first- and third-degree during the filming of his last scene when yellow smoke meant to pour out of his mouth during his death scene overheated (Naha 1984: 103-104). Most of his scenes would be shared with Lady Jessica Atreides, played by Francesca Annis. Her most famous film role prior to *Dune* was as Lady Macbeth in Roman Polanski's box office bomb *Macbeth* of 1971, but she has consistently worked on British television and stage for many decades. She would go on to have a memorable turn as Mrs. Wellington in *Under the Cherry Moon* (Prince, 1986), giving her an unenviable record of having substantial roles in three underappreciated film flops.[9]

One other Atreides character was the source of trouble; Gurney Halleck, Paul's weapons teacher and one of his many mentors. Lynch had originally planned to cast Aldo Ray, a seasoned screen actor typecast as lower-rank military tough guys in film like *Battle Cry* (Raoul Walsh, 1955). Ray struggled with alcoholism during the early phase of production and Patrick Stewart was brought in on very short notice (Godwin 2016: 124). Stewart had already been successful on stage, and was stepping into bigger films roles at the time. Godwin shares an extraordinary moment with Stewart during an interview during *Dune*'s production, one telling, beautiful and absurd:

> …my last major film was in a similar vein, it was *Excalibur* for John Boorman, which was equally an heroic and epic film. I played Leondegrance, who was one of the old warlords, Guinevere's father. [a dog wanders by] Hi, dog. One of our Mexican friends. Cave canem. (Godwin 2016: 330)

Later, Stewart would strengthen his relationship to science fiction and become far more famous for his recurring lead role in *Star Trek: The Next Generation* (1987–1993) as Captain Jean-Luc Picard and the *X-Men* film franchise (2000–2017) as Dr. Charles Xavier. Speaking to Godwin about science fiction in general at the time, Stewart says he enjoyed working on *Dune* because the dialogue was controlled and specific, whereas 'It's so easy to be general, to be vague, particularly when you're dealing with fantasy and science fiction, you can generalize about something' (Godwin 2016: 333).

Casting the lead role of Paul Atreides would take a great deal of time, and accounts vary on the number of screen tests sent to the triumvirate to no avail. Eventually, Jenkins and Lynch expanded the search for young male actors to theatre networks in cities like Seattle. The careful sifting of potential leads finally yielded Kyle MacLachlan, who had never acted for the camera before. MacLachlan met Lynch at his temporary office at Universal Studios in Los Angeles and talked more about the film and the director's plans than his acting. He had adored *Dune* since reading it at the age of

14 and had spent his teenage years relating to Paul Atreides. MacLachlan's role in holding together the dramatic beats of *Dune* can hardly be overstated. As a devoted fan of the book, he balanced Paul's deep intelligence and growing viciousness with his warmth and familial kindness. Godwin recalls seeing MacLachlan before he shot his first ever scene, and asking him if he was playing Paul, to which the young MacLachlan replied 'some of the time' before bouncing off (Godwin 2016: 37).

Greg Olson describes MacLachlan in *Dune* as possessing two imposing acting qualities: 'the agile intelligence behind dark, questing eyes; and his self-contained, serious-minded bearing' (2008: 157). In a flourish of romance, he also muses that MacLachlan connected to *Dune* because of the transformation of the actor's childhood home in the Yakima Valley, which had turned from semi-arid to agricultural land in the second half of the twentieth century, and that 'he could smell the acres of hops and mint around him and fully imagine himself at home in Herbert's fiction' (ibid.). Whatever the reasons for this connection, if MacLachlan had been less serious about the role, or played it with any hint of irony or bravado, *Dune* may have fallen over completely. He is a gentle guide, held together by the growing pressure that engulfs him – despite being emptied of some of the cataclysmic horror that awaits his character's counterpart in the book.

Lynch would later describe MacLachlan as an 'actor who plays innocents who are interested in the mysteries of life' which makes his flashes of anger all the more compelling in *Dune* (Schneller 1992). As Jeffrey Beaumont in *Blue Velvet* and Dale Cooper in *Twin Peaks*, MacLachlan developed his capacity for that innocence; but his adventures through trauma and strange dimensions in all three cases leave him utterly changed.

MacLachlan's collaboration with Lynch is just one of many that emerged from *Dune*. The Harkonnen assassin and Mentat Piter De Vries is played with actor Brad Dourif's usual abandon and relish. Iankin Nefud, played by *Eraserhead*'s Jack Nance, is a subtly dumbstruck figure, twitching with energy – Nance's lifelong friendship with Lynch would take him to further roles in *Blue Velvet*, *Wild at Heart*, *Twin Peaks*, *Twin Peaks: Fire Walk With Me* and *Lost Highway*. The traitor Wellington Yueh is played by Dean Stockwell, who had a long but sporadic career, including an incredible star turn in

Sons and Lovers. In a January 1985 interview, Stockwell recounts that he had been struggling with his career and had all but walked onto the set of *Dune* to ask nicely for a role (Lofficier and Lofficier 1985: 35). Lynch reacted strangely at first, believing Stockwell to be dead – but called for Stockwell when *The Elephant Man*'s star John Hurt, the original Yueh, had a scheduling conflict.[10] A poetically suitable life after death for *Dune*'s traitor. Stockwell, Nance and Dourif would all be reunited in *Blue Velvet* as Ben, Raymond and Paul respectively – guileless lackeys under the spell of Dennis Hopper's unrelenting and torrential Frank Booth.

Dune *alumni in* Blue Velvet: *(from left) Dourif, Nance, MacLachlan and (far right) Stockwell flank J. Michael Hunter, Isabella Rosselini and Dennis Hopper*

The inestimable Freddie Jones, who Lynch had cast in *The Elephant Man* as the horrible Mr. Bytes, the ringmaster who keeps the titular character for his own enrichment, is formidable in *Dune* as Thufir Hawat, the Mentat (a living computer) for House Harkonnen. Jones's long list of credits included Antony and Cleopatra (Peter Snell, 1972) but he would also go on to have roles in *Wild At Heart* (1990) and Lynch's television works, and would later have a 13-year long role on British soap opera *Emmerdale* (1972-present). The universe of *Twin Peaks* was also seeded elsewhere in the cast. Everett McGill had just starred in *Quest for Fire* (Jean-Jacques Annaud, 1981) as the caveman Naoh, and in *Dune* plays Stilgar, a leader among the Fremen. McGill played the fatherly local who knows all the secrets, welcoming the prescient newcomer set to explore all the secrets of the area – similar to McGill's most famous role as Big Ed Hurley in *Twin Peaks* and *Twin Peaks: The Return*. The young child Alia was played by Alicia Witt, who gives the film's ending enough weird childish menace to elevate it to high drama. Witt would go to play Gersten Hayward in *Twin Peaks* and *Twin Peaks: The Return* and has worked continually in film and television roles such as *Cybill* (1995-1998), *Friday Night Lights* (2009-2011) and *Justified* (2014).

Enter Sting. Early in production, the De Laurentiis family worked to add a rockstar to the cast – perhaps remembering the potential Jodorowsky extravaganza. Sting had also appeared in *Brimstone and Treacle* (Richard Loncraine, 1982) and *Quadrophenia* (Franc Roddam, 1979). He had finished recording The Police's fifth and last full studio album *Synchronicity* that February and was on set in Mexico during the weeks in 1983 that the album was released. A biography by Sting's long-time friend Jim Berryman is typical of the excoriation he received about his acting; Berryman's withering aside was that 'after watching some of his other films like *Dune* and *The Bride*, [Berryman] strongly advised him not to forget how to play the guitar' (Berryman 2000: 164). Yet coming after Sting's swaggering performance in Godley and Creme's *Synchroncity II* music video, in which he perches atop a pile of post-apocalyptic rubbish and swings about with teenage fury, Feyd-Rautha is perfectly cast.

Sting, David Lynch and Kyle MacLachlan prepare the final scene (credit: Everett Collection Inc./ Alamy Stock Photo)

The massive cast would be filled out right up to the start of principal photography. Sean Young, playing the Fremen warrior Chani, was famous for her role as Rachael in

Blade Runner (Ridley Scott, 1982) but some of her best roles would come after *Dune*, such as those in *Wall Street* (Oliver Stone, 1987) and *A Kiss Before Dying* (James Dearden, 1991).[11] The Baron's Doctor is played by Leonardo Cimino, a long-time collaborator and friend of José Ferrer, with quiet and undisturbed erotic abandon. His most memorable line 'your diseases, lovingly cared for' is whispered right into the Baron's pustules. The Baron himself is played by Kenneth McMillan who had appeared in films including *Little Miss Marker* (Walter Bernstein, 1980), *Eyewitness* (Peter Yates, 1981) and Stuart Rosenberg's *The Pope of Greenwich Village* in the same year *Dune* was released.

In the weeks of May and June 1983, Lynch was overseeing some of the largest creative decisions across the production. A much-discussed but relatively secretive aspect of production is the soundtrack, developed by Toto. The band's keyboardist David Paich performed much of the arranging and composing across the score; while his father Marty Paich conducted the Vienna Symphony Orchestra and the Vienna Volksoper Choir to accompany the band. While in retrospect, critics like Theirry Jousse call this 'proggy' effect 'catastrophically awful' (Jousse 2010: 28), that is largely due to one of the tracks, the 'Desert Theme', whereas *Dune*'s sobriety and intensity is reinforced by the more languid background tracks. Eighteen months before the film was released, Godwin interviewed Lynch about the film and began with questions about the soundtrack. Lynch lets slip that Gilbert Marouani – the music producer who was then helping to organise the soundtrack – had come to Lynch 'with very bad news that no one wants to work on the project' and that the list of possible composers and collaborators was by then becoming exhausted (Godwin 2016: 276).

Lynch wanted to develop a mix of orchestral and synthesised music, triggered by a discussion with the members of Toto who had visited the day before – and in *The Guardian* interview also discusses an approach to Brian Eno that is yet to take place. Eno is credited with the 'Prophecy Theme' addition to the soundtrack – a lilting, smooth synth arrangement that is used during some key moments of revelation. Rumours that he composed a full soundtrack for the film that was rejected have never been confirmed, but a transcript from a 1988 radio show seems to indicate that Daniel Lanois, Roger Eno and Brian Eno (the same lineup as their album *Apollo: Atmospheres and Soundtracks* in 1983) worked a single track up from a 'waltz' into its current form, with no mention of a longer project (Enoweb.co.uk 2017). Lynch wanted to have different sonic textures for the planets to match their visual differences – which even the soundtrack's most ardent defenders would say isn't quite there in the final release.[12] What both Toto and Eno added above all was pure star power. As inelegant as that explanation is, it is part of the *Dune* production story – to assemble a galaxy of the best and brightest, in order to elevate the film well past its constraints.

With a lineup of talent and experience this profound, *Dune*'s pre-production could not have had more going for it. Experienced actors, many with deep stage experience, and old masters behind the camera provide the basis for the excellent performances and masterful production elements. But one fateful decision by Raffaella De Laurentiis, crucial to *Dune*'s story, changed the film at its core.

ALL EYES TURNED TO ARRAKIS

That decision, made in mid-June 1983, was to switch the entire special effects production of the film. Initially, it was to be based in a state-of-the-art facility in Los Angeles, which was being headed up by John Dykstra (*Star Wars*, *Star Trek: The Motion Picture* [Robert Wise, 1979], *Battlestar Galactica*) and his company Apogee. Raffaella De Laurentiis was greatly concerned that each time a camera was turned on in Los Angeles, it would cost over $30,000, and wanted the capacity to reshoot scenes if Lynch wished without blowing out the budget (Naha 1984: 209-210). This decision was taken after prop work, effects preparation and minor special effects sequence production had already begun. To replace them, Raffaella brought together a team to work in Mexico: her 'family', her 'people'. Barry Nolan from Van Der Veer Photo Effects would take over, alongside a team of effects experts with different specialisms. *Dune* was and remains Nolan's only special effects credit (although he had extensive work experience in visual effects as an effects animator on *Star Wars* and a special photographic effects assistant on *Flash Gordon* in 1980). Julie Turnock analysed the De Laurentiis special effects approach at this time, noting 'ambitious and lavishly designed production is often undermined by cost-cutting at the optical printing level' (2012: 140).

This disrupted process – involving the layering of matte backgrounds, slow motion shots, dissolves, fades and overlays – was crucial to *Dune*'s eventual finished form. What we are left with is richly layered, but frayed at the edges. It wasn't just cost-cutting, however – it was also an attempt to maintain independence from the increasingly atomised and specialised studio effects systems that were beginning to dominate. In an interview with Godwin at the time of production, when Dykstra was still involved in the project and otherwise optimistic, he noted that he had an 'embarrassment of riches with regard to the story and an embarrassment of poverty with regard to the money' (2016: 361). In this interview, Bob Bealman (Apogee Inc.'s supervisor on the project) and Dykstra himself are hopeful that they're heading towards an innovative mix of optical and other effects techniques to deliver on the promise of the film's setting and script. Dykstra is excited about using timing variances and miniatures to shoot wide shots of deserts (2016: 359). It's clear Dykstra wanted the film to succeed as an effects piece but also speaks to its reputation and the aura of the *Dune* universe:

> *Dune* is very special. I mean, I think even within this business, the people who make special effects for sure, because it's tied into science fiction, but even people who make films in general know that this movie is a very special movie. It has that sense about it. The producer has that sense about her. The director has that sense about him. (Godwin 2016: 362)

This was a time of tremendous upheaval in other ways: apart from the effects team being replaced completely, in the coming crucial months, Lynch was guiding the filming and editing of a film he felt even by then just wasn't working, and Churubusco Studios would expand its focus – perhaps too broadly – to accommodate the second *Conan* film, *Conan the Destroyer*, also being produced by Raffaella. Michel Chion even cites French pre-release press that claimed while the *Dune* was shooting on one side of a sand dune, Conan was wrestling barbarians on the other (2006: 75).[13]

Special effects artist Carlo Rambaldi came to the project as creature effect leader after his Oscar wins for both *Alien* and *E.T. The Extra-Terrestrial*. His Guild Navigator, gestating Alia and mechanical special effects were headed up by Kit West, whose role is extensively covered in the Naha book. Going through the various challenging effects – the Baron's wire-work, the hunter-seeker missile that attempts to kill Paul – there is a complexity and ingenuity to the effects production that is impressive.[14]

This leads to the one set of eyes through which this story is most clearly told: the film's cinematographer Freddie Francis. With a career as both a cinematographer and director, in the former his credits include *Sons and Lovers*, *The Innocents* (Jack Clayton, 1961) and *The French Lieutenant's Woman*, while in the latter capacity he would direct a number of genre films for British horror studios Hammer and Amicus, later returning to work with Lynch on *The Straight Story* (1999). If Lynch has expressed misgivings and regrets about *Dune* over the years, Francis was more unequivocal: 'a classic it most certainly isn't' and that the film 'had little cohesion and was painfully sluggish' (Francis 2013: 198, 199). In his 2013 autobiography, Francis outlines the experience of joining the project, and planning and executing its cinematography with a focus on the desert scenes in particular. His recollections centre on wanting to help Lynch make a memorable science fiction adventure movie, but he wasn't impressed by Lynch's screenplay early on and warned him to do more research and preparation:

> My main concern was that I was very conscious all the time that the progress and the action were much, much too slow. You cannot make a four-hour time and then cut it to two hours and believe it will be any faster. (Francis 2013: 199)

Francis reinforces the same overall impressions of the relationship between Lynch and the De Laurentiis family that both Naha and Godwin provide: that while amicable, their visions of how the film should look and feel were never unified. But Francis did what he could: one of his innovations was to introduce a 'Lightflex' device onto the cameras, a box mounted on the front with convex Perspex and a row of lights shining inward. This allowed for far great control over contrast and allowed muted tones to be built up in otherwise busy shots (2016: 193). He mentions that the shadows in the desert were built up to be brown instead of black to convey it is an alien environment (2016: 200).

Among Francis's many frustrations were that set designs were constructed under orders of Lynch and Tony Masters prior to him arriving in Mexico, and many of the sets and miniatures had been built without consideration for moving a big camera rig around these environments. This practically limited his options for basic lens choices and lengthened the time it took for what should, from his perspective, have been otherwise simple shots (2016: 201). But perhaps the most 'uncreative and frustrating' element for Francis was the lack of control over the actual look of many of the shots – they would be bundled across to a complicated effects department and he would have no idea how they'd look in the final version.

Across all the available material on *Dune*'s production, there remains an impression that many of the most complex sequences were achingly close to looking far richer, more developed, and less flimsy that what finally ended up on screen. Despite his inexperience, Barry Nolan's overall optical work is not to blame, as there are several excellent shots in the final version and other elements described in Naha's book and elsewhere that emphasise the quality and importance of his contribution. Nolan himself seemed to have been aware that the production was losing traction. Late in production, when asked how he would describe the critical worm scenes, Nolan is blunt: 'I wouldn't' (Naha 1984: 282). As important as the special effects decision was, and the negative impact it would have on the film's final look, it's hard to conclude that it was the wrong call. With the spiralling costs of special effects at the top end of the industry, pressure across the industry to elevate the science fiction form, a dizzying script by an art-house darling aching for more control, and an immense cast already in place, Raffaella's decision probably averted a genuine financial disaster. *Dune*'s final form – all physical effects, with all the vicissitudes of old-school epic film-making – shows its seams throughout, but it holds together like an ancient machine being put through its paces one last time. Watching *Dune* is an exercise in a different kind of suspended disbelief, where we are asked to have faith in the excesses not regarding the onscreen fiction, but the fantasy of film production itself, like a stage curtain being pulled aside in deep space.

Footnotes

4. All references to the *Dune* shooting scripts in this book are entirely thanks to Duneinfo.com, maintained by Mark Bennett.

5. Intriguingly, Paul M. Sammon reveals Scott was interested in fusing themes and images from Gillo Pontecorvo's *The Battle of Algiers* (1966) with the *Dune* material (Sammon 1996).
6. Dino's production career also dipped into comic culture's pop aesthetic as it emerged, and included two cherished cult films, Mario Bava's *Danger: Diabolik* and Roger Vadim's *Barbarella*, filmed back-to-back and both released in 1968. These included sadomasochistic costumes and pop art elements, rooted in the comic book origins of each film. The sadomasochism and comic silliness would return in *Flash Gordon* (Mike Hodges, 1980) through a deliriously high camp lens.
7. One of *Dune*'s public mysteries is the presence of dogs and especially pugs. Possible inspirations for Lynch's sudden decision may be the high number of dogs in Mexico City, the outdoor set nicknamed 'Dead Dog Dump', Jurgen Prochnow's pet who had come to the set with him – beautifully detailed in an interview in the 2016 Godwin diary. As explained in Chapter Three, there's an art history context for their presence as well.
8. Longer scenes were cut where he would have been responsible for demonstrating Fremen traditions.
9. A horrible coincidence would connect the actors playing the elder Atreides. In October 1983, Francesca Annis shared an extraordinary anecdote about being severely burned during a gas explosion at her rented villa while filming *Dune*, treated with the hospital's last tube of burn cream remaining from treating earlier victims of an air disaster (Davis 1983).
10. Stockwell had spent time off-screen selling real estate in New Mexico when he and his wife travelled to Mexico for a vacation; his casting was a story of happenstance and luck.
11. Sean Young uploaded a six-minute behind-the-scenes video of *Dune* filmed on Super 8 in 2010 to YouTube, showing the cast relaxing in between takes.
12. Most interestingly, it's Godwin who begins this entire discussion by mentioning Krzysztof Penderecki as a rumoured collaborator, and Lynch would eventually use a very long segment of that composer's 'Thernody for the Victims of Hiroshima' in the centrepiece episode of *Twin Peaks: The Return* in 2017. While it's only a small link, it's not altogether silly to imagine that the seed of that episode was planted in Mexico.
13. The Naha and Godwin books have dozens of eye-opening anecdotes about the production environment being out of control. To feed the international cast and crew, Raffaella hired a full-time pasta chef from Italy only to find out that Mexican authorities were more than willing to impound pasta in customs for months (Lim 2015: 62).
14. Others, which West explains in excited detail (like the film's concluding explosion where the Baron spins in mid-air, and an explosion outside causes both him and Alia Atreides to be sucked out of an imploded wall) ended up looking more than just merely dated after they were assembled optically; they look visually broken, unmade, even uncanny (Naha 1984: 152-154).

3. MIND IN MOTION: WATCHING *DUNE*

With the benefit of hindsight, viewing *Dune* is still a slow and serene experience. Critical readings of *Dune* have often noted how dense its unexplained setting was compared to films like *Star Wars*, *Alien* and the *Star Trek* films. Yet this supposed density makes it feel quaint and distant, and watching it in the twenty-first century in terms of its film language alone is at times akin to watching old serials of the 1920s and 1930s. Actors are given languid speeches in dense scenes; strange and unpleasant moments are granted as much screen time as the film's core science fiction cornerstones; the worms, the stillsuits, the weirding modules.

In each case, Lynch builds a soft and fungible symbolic order to replace the encyclopaedic, literary version. This 'soft symbolism' is malleable; taking on board what we know of Lynch's approach to matter, the dream sequences refer forward and backward like any other, but also are there to take pure pleasure in form and arrangement. This is Lynchian science fiction. At the very moment *Dune* was bombing at the United States box office (but still going strong in Europe), Lynch reflected on an 'ideal' cinema:

> The ideal I'm talking about would have dialogue coming in like music and sitting within a bed of sound effects. Sound and image would be designed as part of the whole but the whole would be greater than the sum of its parts. You would have reached the magic combination and be transported. (Lewis 1985: 8)

This observation is the blueprint for how I approach this chapter. *Dune*'s final form is acute with montages, voice-overs, interludes, inter-cuts and fades in this fashion. A close analysis is best done attuned to the film's unusual structure; speeding up where the material is loosely arranged and paying strict attention where the film demands it. As I argue, the first third of the film has more to say than the last third. It is clear across past analyses of the film that critics and academics have often relied on alternate cuts and editions as they write. While my own close analysis will refer to the Alan Smithee version and excised material where relevant, this chapter relies on the 137-minute theatrical version – not because it is Lynch's, but because much of the push to produce alternative cuts comes from an abiding love with the novel and its universe. This book concerns the bombastic and sometimes subterranean hidden power of the existing film.

This close analysis privileges texture and attenuation as much as narrative and character. There are, simply put, some parts of the film with a great deal written about them which require more time to properly account for – and also entire passages of the film which past critics have flagged as meaningless, confusing and arbitrary. Some DVD and Blu-ray chapter divisions of the film begin with several 15-20-minute chapters, and then speed up to many more 4-7 minute chapters – an inconvenient structure, even for machines, but revealing in terms of how content within the film is structurally conceived. This isn't a structural imbalance; rather, imbalance is the structure. Michel Chion's extraordinary book on Lynch delves into this and retrieves another analysis:

> Where Lynch has been most audacious has been the structuring of the story. He devised a kind of spiralling structure, described by him as circular, in which all the information needed to understand the story is given from the start rather than being doled out progressively. ... *Dune* is thus Lynch's first effort at feature-length, non-linear narration. (Chion 2005: 65)

Chion isn't being defensive; he is referencing quotes given by Lynch to *Starfix Magazine* and *L'ecran Fantastique Magazine* (both in French). In those interviews, Lynch gave strikingly different responses than those he gave anywhere in English. If the *structure* of the film is indeed spiralling or circular as Chion suggests, then it explains a great deal not only about the story, but about the entire breadth of affect it brings to the viewer. There is a structural reason, then, why scenes at the beginning are more intense, shot more closely, and are dense with meaning. Paul's dreams cut through the spiral structure by introducing later important elements earlier in the film. Following Paul and his mother's escape from the Harkonnen attack midway through the film, *Dune*'s attitude towards us changes in the tone and narrative structure most of all. By film's end, we have entered a state of what can only be described as *permanent and total montage*. It's not *change* in some amorphous sense, but an *observable structural quality* of the film itself.

To underscore the importance of this fundamental but widely ignored structural aspect, this chapter spirals and turns in its own way. As the film progresses, we approach the initial opening scenes meticulously and with the strictest attention because this is where the film *itself* is the most meticulous and attentive. Moving with the film itself, I will progressively spiral outward to look to aspects of production where the film is most sensible and readable through that lens. As the gyre widens, the battle sequences are rendered relatively and deliberately mute in *Dune*, while character exchanges are brought forward. This analysis of *Dune* is therefore focussed on what makes the film special; the science fiction of intense relationships, the deep space of ominous close-ups, the mystical forces inside people.

A VERY DELICATE TIME

Dune opens on Princess Irulan's epigraph; actor Virginia Madsen glides out of the starlight gloom, with every indication is that she is just a narrator, half angelic herald and half distracted usher. The image is a direct bridge to the final shot of *The Elephant Man*, which faded into the stars on the spectral face of John Merrick's mother, welcoming him into death with words from Lord Tennyson's poem 'Nothing Will Die'. We re-enter the Lynch film universe four years later with an actor announcing life; a collage of *Dune*'s plot elements and the central figure yet to be revealed. Madsen's airy faux-British diction gives Princess Irulan a distant authority over proceedings. She reveals it is the Year 10,191, briefly outlining the major forces in the galaxy, and then mentions that the spice expands consciousness. She fades out into the stars only to return two second later with additional information – about the Spacing Guild and their ability to fold space. She disappears once more to return again briefly with a jaunty 'Oh yes, I forgot to tell you – the spice exists on only one planet in the entire universe', and then continues into the more ominous prophecies of the Fremen.

Nochimson says that Irulan's 'dignity is comically undermined' by this fading in and out, using an 'oops' effect that sets the film up almost as a farce (1997: 126). Todd McGowan agrees this fading undercuts Irulan's position, undoing the usual work of a narrator, but also noting that Irulan's fragments throughout *Dune* are reassuring and

Last shot of The Elephant Man *(top) and first shot of* Dune

stabilising (2007: 76). McGowan refers to Chion in the process, reminding us this instability is not aimed at Irulan, but the whole film universe, especially since the idea of 'voice' is essentially a truth-making superpower as the story progresses. Irulan is therefore serious but unstable, dramatic but unreliable.

An attractive alternative reading is that Irulan's fading reads like an interrupted signal. Lines cut from this scene in editing (which would have involved more fading in and out) expanded on the Bene Gesserit sisterhood, explained the Mentats and the lack of computers ('thinking machines') and given Irulan even less authority since her character would be grounded, her position in the sisterhood revealed.[15]

The shots at the end of *The Elephant Man* echoed in Madsen's introduction to Dune are reminiscent of Lillian Gish in the prologue to *The Night of the Hunter* (Charles Laughton, 1955) but also have deep roots in the *Dune* novel's structures. What we have left of Irulan – this epigraph, scattered voice-overs and a few short moments in the film proper – is an attempt to articulate her far more important role in the books.

In the first *Dune* book, she provides structural integrity to the interweaving threads, and returns us to the same imperious position with a new epigraph excerpt at the beginning of each chapter. In the film, she is a signal from *outside* the text – perhaps resonating as another 'voice from the outer world'. While this term has special value in the *Dune* mythos, it also importantly prefigures *Twin Peaks*' 'man from another place'. Because her epigraph is quite indistinct, the viewer is drawn to two words in her lines. First, simply 'mutated', in reference to the Guild Navigators, and 'messiah' in reference to the Kwisatch Haderach, pronounced with a brief flourish of theatrical zealotry.

A strange computer speaks to us

After Irulan's introduction, *Dune*'s prog-rock sonic textures are established over the title sequence; Toto's 'Main Title' track is brassy, portentous and broad. The titles are simple – etched serif font in all capitals, perfectly in keeping with a science fiction film made by a production company with deep roots in the Biblical epic tradition. Immediately after the titles, we're taken to a sparse, unfeeling computer display and a disembodied voice announces 'A Secret Report Within the Guild'. After Irulan's warning and the titles' brash pronouncements, it's like being dropped into a cold bath. A field of black stars is overlaid with a faint white grid, an explaining-computer. The four planets of Arrakis, Caladan, Giedi Prime and Kaitain are displayed, seemingly as flat pictures. The overall effect feels modern and austere even today; the font displaying the planet names is widely spaced, like an ancient regal system is letting us peer inside, rather than the functional mix of data and visualisation typical of *Star Wars* or *Star Trek: The Motion Picture*.

This sequence is the subject of some secrecy and confusion in press and critical considerations of *Dune* but has emerged as one of the most iconic and well-remembered images in the film. In an insert caption in the September 1984 issue of *Cinefantastique Magazine*, two beautiful half-spherical models meant for this sequence and painted by Ron Miller are photographed, along with an explanation that they were unable to be used due to the 'crude equipment' available at Churubusco, requiring them to be re-done as flat art (Sammon 1984: 77). It seems inconsequential, but the simple logoform of the Guild (also designed by Miller) of three spheres with a single connecting line is one of the film's most enduring, enigmatic images. It's a computer, but not in a way we know them to behave on film. It isn't depicted as neutral and informative, but as coolly magisterial.

PLANET KAITAIN

As we arrive on Kaitain, the ship lands in the foreground against the Emperor's building in the background. This immense wooden model was constructed late in production during January 1984, and stands approximately eight-to-nine feet tall. The quality of the light entering the lens and the descending ship miniature are our first taste of the actual 'effects' sequences of *Dune*, and they look diminished, unfinished and haphazard. Their intended effect of a dreary, cold, unfeeling cosmos consciously avoids the 'slick' qualities of contemporary films. It's in this opening sequence that we see all of *Dune*'s dreamlike promise and visual quirks. The first thing we see is the gleaming golden room of the Emperor's throne room; by far the film's most striking interior. Aside from this spectacle, in these few short minutes, we see arranged the forces active within the plot as The Emperor receives the Third Stage Guild Navigator, reveals his intent to betray House Atreides, and in return the Navigator warns the Emperor to deal with Paul before an unknown problem emerges.

Dennis Lim described this room as a 'baroque explosion of gold, dripping in Moorish honeycomb patterns' (2015: 62). But it's Martha Nochimson's first book on Lynch which best attempted to give voice to seeing this intricate environment, calling it 'bewilderingly carnivalized' and noting that it is both 'ornate and shallow, as if a full-sized cathedral were constructed of thin metallic plate' (Nochimson 1997: 127).

Irulan leaves the ornate throne room of her father, the Emperor

Godwin attempts a description by calling this set part of 'the first art nouveau science fiction film, with Spanish detailing added' (2016: 38). This influence is an important one: *Dune*'s primary matte illustrator Ron Miller captioned an early production painting of this room as inspired by the Alhambra palatial complex in Granada, Spain (Duneinfo.com). This is especially obvious in its Hall of the Abencerrajes, where golden light arcs around and inside honeycombed vaulting. Part fortress, part palace, this complex is the best-known example of late Muslim art and architecture in Europe. Built in the thirteenth century as part of the Nasrid Emirate of Granada, it was heavily altered and fortified in later centuries, and then re-adopted in the Renaissance idiom to house the court of Ferdinand and Isabella when the Emirate was expelled from the Iberian Peninsula.[16]

In the film, our first look at the throne room is framed by honeycombing up the walls, and carved lions which give it a showy, theatrical look. Flooded lighting across back areas and curved walls foreshortens the room. It's also a court in action; the camera pans, catching social movements. Officials mill about the seated Emperor, a doghandler rushes past with nine stout little dogs on leashes, the gold of the walls is contrasted with the emerald green floor and sparse furniture. Big, brash Hollywood costume dramas, Dino De Laurentiis epics and war films are all part of the visual language in this scene; slow pans move across a complex set of characters, and frames the room into thirds on both the vertical and horizontal plane. An alarm starts when we see the doghandler; a loud, grinding tone which is perhaps the only science fiction element in the environment, to begin with at least.

It is only once the shock of the absurd detailing has worn off that the blend of costume elements comes into focus. As Vivian Sobchack notes, in this scene '*Dune* stands as the costume museum, its spatial collection of 16th-and 19th- century dress a sign of the narrative's temporal weakness, fragmentation and paralysis' (1987: 263). While not everyone is as disappointed as Sobchack, ideas of fragmentation and paralysis are useful when reading these heavily costumed scenes – invoking what she calls a 'hermetic and temporally paralyzing materiality' (1987: 263). The Emperor has a jewelled cloak over a dark sashed military uniform, while attendants and officials mix with the more brutal black Sardukar inflated bodysuits. Almost all the women are in flowing gowns with black lace veils. Only Irulan, veritably bedazzled in gold and white in a beautifully shot exchange with her father, seems to be privileged by the camera, particularly in a shot that follows her from the left of the scene and then cuts into a receded foreground, welcoming her into a side passage. The 'veiled, bejeweled, overdressed' women in this scene evoke a clash of styles, from the Elizabethan court, to Spanish and Flemish painting (Nochimson 1997: 127).

This first court scene contains an astonishing aesthetic melange. It reminds us of nothing specific, but is yet still eerily familiar. It's serious science fiction, but the artificial quality is so startling that it approaches the visual texture of *Flash Gordon* as much as *2001*. Angela Ndalianis has delved deeply into the connection between science fiction and what she coined the 'neo-baroque'; her term for the playful collapse of visual and sensory paradoxes in contemporary visual culture, part of which is an invitation to the viewer to take part in these paradoxes (2011: 40). *Dune* is explicitly built using a collapsed Renaissance as a reference point, and Lynch's trip to Venice with the De Laurentiis family looms large in the film's pre-history. But this is something else – artificial, severe, bombastic.

Yet it is just a warm up. *Dune*'s most startling and visually memorable moment is the arrival of the Third Stage Guild Navigator. Honeycombed doors slide apart with an uneven jagged pattern; they look like the tinted brass of an old key rather than luxurious gold. The fish-eye lens warps, allowing the backwards-tracking shot to reveal more of the room. There is no music, and thus a quiet kind of paranoia is created rather than the grandiose energy it would have with a soundtrack. The immense black tank rolls in, flanked by the bald, black Guildsmen – the tank is at the centre of the distorted lens, fifteen feet high and fifty feet long – our celebrated and feared interdimensional breadbin. The Navigator's striking presence almost didn't happen: *Dune*'s creature effects expert Carlo Rambaldi was interviewed both days of this scene's filming, lamenting that the Navigator had trouble folding real space – half of its head collapsed during the truck ride to Mexico, and it required remaking (Naha 1984: 238).

As the Guildsmen demand that the 'Bene Gesserit witch must leave', we see the Reverend Mother retreat to a side room to use her psychic scrying powers and *Dune* is announcing here how different it wants to be. When the mechanism on the front of the tank unlocks, we cut to the Reverend Mother, then back to the tank, then to the Emperor – a tense stand-off amplified by the blazing gold and smoky black. The tank reveals a miasma of orange spice dust, and we are given our first look at the bloated, brainy Navigator. Vivian Sobchack noted that the Navigator is 'literally, gigantically "sluggish" – and hermetically sealed in the controlled atmosphere of what appears to be an old museum display case' (Sobchack 1987: 278). But as quickly as the shock of the creature comes, so does its pulping, pumping, fleshy, flap-valve mouth. J. Hoberman famously described the grotesquery on display when we see the creature as 'a withered vulva (typically shown in tight close-up) complete with clitoris' (1991: 207). It has the same visual discomfort as the *Eraserhead* baby, but acts like a disfigured nude delivering threats like a Mafia hitman from the window of a passing car. José Ferrer's idiom in *Dune* is sometimes criticised for being overly stagey; stuttering, exaggerated head movements and nervous diction – but for those familiar with his earlier work, even just a few minutes into this scene, the skills of an old master are on full display. He shrugs off the robe and pouts with false bravado as he awaits the arrival of the menacing Third Stage Guild Navigator. Only five minutes into *Dune*, the film's most consequential exchange is now set up. The severe but kindly Reverend Mother Gaius Helen Mohiam (Sîan Phillips) makes her first appearance to reassure and warn the Emperor. Together, we're alerted to their power relationship. He, the tin-pot dictator, and she the glaring vizier.

The Navigator is often compared to *Star Wars*' Jabba in terms of design, but according to the visual logic of *Dune*, it's closer to the Death Star. But after 2017 and *Twin Peaks: The Return*, perhaps the closest analogue is the fate of Phillip Jeffries, a figure who folds space and time, steam and all, inside an oily black machine.

Navigators of time and space; Twin Peaks: The Return *(top) and* Dune

This sequence was filmed on September 9, 1983. As the Emperor shrugs off his cloak, and assures the Guild Navigator that they are alone, Lynch would say 'cut' and *Dune* would conclude principal photography – this sequence was among the last filmed, perhaps accounting for its confidence, energy and meticulous feel.[17]

PLANET CALADAN

When we first shift to the planetary home of House Atreides, Irulan's voice explains more of the Bene Gesserit's plans as waves crash in the dark at the foot of a mighty fortress. We are quickly introduced to Paul Atreides, using his 'filmbook': the polar inverse of our kind of computer, it is shown in such a way to continue our introduction to the many elements yet in play – the Mentats, Arrakis, spice mining, Carryalls, the worms and, finally, the Harkonnen and their Baron's need to take the ducal signet ring from Paul's father. All of this is expansively over-explained, as each element is later revisited both visually and verbally.

The purpose of this scene is to introduce us to Gurney (Patrick Stewart), Dr. Yueh (Dean Stockwell) and Thufir Hawat (Freddie Jones) as Paul's mentors, teachers and friends. Gurney challenges Paul to a training duel, reminding him sternly that he needn't be in the mood for fighting, since 'mood's a thing for cattle and loveplay.' A fight sequence between them with awkward prismatic effects hiding the details of the action means we focus on Paul's inner voice as he speculates about Gurney's motivations. The visual effect communicates they have personal shields to protect them, but it also literally hides the action beneath a blurred set of shifting boxes. At the stalemate conclusion of their duel, the visual of the shield is stable and we see it shimmering, a watery effect, moving like waves inside prismatic shapes. After the duel, their mentoring takes us through several more plot points, and segues into the second training sequence, when Thufir demands that they 'activate a fighter'.

It's here that we see the dark wooden carving work common to all Caladan interiors at their most elegant. The room looks utterly ancient, and the brass training unit emerges to a mild rhythmic thrumming from the soundtrack. While the scene is nominally comparable to Luke learning how to use a lightsaber on the Millennium Falcon with his visor down against a training droid, or to a martial arts training dummy like those made famous by Bruce Lee, it also sits neatly in the Lynch technological tradition. Obscure, obtuse, ornate, orthogonal; another brass and gold machine would appear in 2017 in *Twin Peaks: The Return*, as part of a heavily stylised sequence in the 'White Lodge' plane – one of several visual matches to Caladan in other Lynch work.

To fight the machine, Yueh fits Paul with his 'weirding module' – one of Lynch's own additions to the plot. Although controversial to Herbert fans, this device attached to Paul's neck works well to visualise an abstraction – his vocal powers – but in a style that's itself abstract, unclear. The visual design of Caladan is as far from science fiction as audiences could have expected. Production designer Tony Masters remarked that everything they designed for Caladan and its characters had to look 'very functional. Ugly if necessary, lumpy and awkward but functional' (Naha 1984: 52). In both positive and negative senses, that goal was certainly accomplished.

Brass machines in the ceiling: Twin Peaks: The Return *(top) and* Dune

It's a later conversation between Paul and his father the Duke that gives us the film's first emotional texture, standing in contrast with a steady stream of tense plot beats. Paul meets his father at night, overlooking the dark night seas of Caladan, in which we first hear the resonant mantra that will recur several times throughout the film: 'the sleeper must awaken.' The Duke's simple reminder to his son sets up the later sorrow; the film puts Leto's death at the centre of Paul's journey in this moment. While Martha Nochimson accuses the phrase of too much 'overripe authority' (1997: 130), Todd McGowan instead focusses on Paul's face in this scene as indicating 'the prospect of him awakening into a new world' (2007: 74). But this moment centres on Prochnow's dour, sad delivery – our romantic and gallant figure on the way to his fate, flags waving in the night.

As much as devout fans and Lynch himself like to quarantine his other work from *Dune*, this moment is explicitly evoked in *Twin Peaks: The Return*. This series in part hinges around the anticipation of MacLachlan's iconic Agent Cooper being released

The sleeper must awaken; Twin Peaks: The Return *(top) and* Dune

from his interdimensional prison, the mystical 'Black Lodge' zone-between-zones around which key moments in the original series also centred. In *The Return*, Cooper is spat out from the Lodge onto a ledge overlooking a deep purple sea. The Black Lodge is part hotel lobby, part antechamber to the infinite, and Cooper's escape from it is the entire premise of the new series. There's Good Cooper (stuck in there) and Bad Cooper (out in the world we know). This purple sea comes as a sensory and narrative shock, as an environment new to *Twin Peaks*. The mythology of the series has suddenly and violently expanded: we know of the White Lodge, heard hints at a greater cosmology as the original series wound down (largely without Lynch's active involvement). Cooper looks out over these crashing waves, on the verge of beginning a journey that will take him through several cosmic stages before beginning a suburban odyssey as Dougie, half-insensate and searching for a way to fully awaken as Cooper.

For fans of *Dune*, who have for decades been resigned to Lynch's disavowal of the film, this moment amounts to nothing less than a direct taunt. MacLachlan's Paul is given that ominous advice from his father – 'the sleeper must awaken' – later repeated to Cooper/Dougie with almost sacred intensity as 'wake up' by his mystical guide figure, Mike (Al Strobel).[18] It may not be on Lynch's agenda to revisit *Dune* thematically; but these repeated visual motifs are no coincidence. The disavowals mean nothing if Lynch keeps returning us to the edge of the water, as MacLachlan watches the same infinite waves.

Paul's first challenge on his new journey is a cerebral showdown. In a highly charged sequence, after Jessica is admonished for giving birth to a boy, the Reverend Mother Gaius Helen Mohiam seeks to assess Paul's control and ability – she summons him ominously to a chamber and asks him to place a hand into the box. If he moves his hand, she'll kill him immediately. Lynch's deft touch with montage is applied here to show what Paul's mind's eye sees – his burning hand that we suspect may not be real – and he is successful. Todd McGowan describes it as our realisation that the 'real threats and the real enjoyment are elsewhere' – an early signal that *Dune*'s phantasmagorias will be illusory (ibid.)

Paul's physical closeness to the Reverend Mother gives the scene a potent weirdness, made all the stranger as we retreat into his inner voice to hear the 'Litany Against Fear', another mantra: 'I must not fear; fear is the mind-killer; fear is the little death that brings total obliteration; I will permit it to pass over me and through me.' The scene is uneasy and charged. As Olson puts it, this exchange has power because 'their heads almost touching, their emotions seething with almost unbearable intensity, confront one another' (2008: 168). His release from this exchange is in new knowledge – the Reverend Mother half-describes the 'water of life' concept from the novel, and makes it all the more intense by explaining that one day, it will allow access for the Kwisatch Haderach to go to a place 'terrifying to women'. The quasi-sexual intimacy of their exchange is still astonishing after dozens of viewings; a searing imprint that confirms your suspicions that the film has more intensity to come.

Paul endures the tension and lets the fear pass 'over him and through him'

PLANET GIEDI PRIME

As we enter Giedi Prime, we're exposed immediately to some of the film's most memorable shots; the immense and imposing 'Face Burner', a grid wall of green lights against steel, and an intricate matte composite of a skyline tram being shunted into frame. Cubes of open-roof green-walled rooms, steam vents and archaic mechanisms foreground a metropolis of sinister inhumanity.[19] To punctuate our introduction, we have shots of Harkonnen officers and staff with shaved heads in an obscure tonsure, stitched-together ears, insinuations of removed eyes and organs.

Greg Olson describes Giedi Prime as the most Lynchian of the planets, noting that 'factories touch Lynch's soul, giving him intimations of cosmic workings' (Olson 2008: 175-176). Olson likens the environment to *The Wizard of Oz* (Victor Fleming et al., 1939) and an old municipal building, to which we can perhaps add the reassuring high-gloss and grime of a London Tube or Paris Metro station (2008: 177). For production designer Tony Masters, Giedi Prime looks 'rather like the inside of Victoria Station with the steam boilers and goodness knows what going on at once' (Naha 1984: 52). Lynch mentally constructed his image of Giedi Prime in that famous trip to Venice with the De Laurentiis family. Experiencing that city at night provided him with an opening gambit in the development of ideas, where he passed through buildings that had 'a very cold light deep within' and 'didn't seem like there were doors' (Godwin 2016: 279).

The grimy industrial tramways and open labyrinth of Giedi Prime

The constellation of Harkonnen characters inhabiting this 'cold light deep within' is presented in near-comical abandon. Godwin was unsure of the casting of McMillan as the Baron, concerned he would be a 'good actor, but totally without a threatening presence' (Godwin 2016: 44). But McMillan brings unyielding brutality, pompous cruelty and sadistic self-regard, although the softness Godwin saw remains – there is a quiet and reflective 'inner voice' moment that is barely whispered, once his dominance is established.

Our introduction to the Harkonnen begins darkly enough, but soon becomes pitch black. A young boy (Ernesto Laguardia) is brought into the room to tend to flowers, and witnesses the Baron declaring his plans to his nephews. When the Baron uses his suspensor suit to fly around the room, and then bathes in oil dripping from the ceiling, as McGowan notes 'Lynch shoots this scene so as to emphasize the sexual dimension of the experience' (2007: 80). The Baron spots the boy, and grabs him roughly, caresses him and then pulls out a plug on his chest, from which his life's blood spurts out in volume, a 'heartplug' in the film's parlance. Kenneth McMillan's voice comes in at a whisper as he speaks directly to us – 'This is what I'll do to the Duke and his family' – as Sting's Feyd Rautha looks on gleefully.

It is, by any account, a scene of total and uninhibited exploitation. It shows cruelty, viciousness, and the low price of life for these characters, cheaply played off against the apparent effeminacy of the murdered boy. All of a sudden, the Baron's pustules bubble with an unabashed fear and fetishisation of disease – tackily drawing down public fear of the AIDS epidemic. Film critic Robin Wood calls *Dune* 'the most obscenely homophobic film [he has] ever seen', referencing this sequence in particular, and highlighting that it connects homosexuality to 'physical grossness, moral depravity, violence and disease' (1986: 174). The fact that the novel's Baron is an outright rapist does this scene no favours; but it is *how* the scene works, not *what* it depicts, that is just as careless. McMillan revealed in an interview with *Enterprise Incidents* that Laguardia wasn't told when the heartplug would be pulled out, leaving the reaction to be ad-libbed (Fischer 1985: 32). Only Jack Nance's Nefud registers any negative reaction. Greg Olson says there's a theme at play here that runs through Lynch's filmography: 'The dark dance between villainy and homosexuality swirls through five of nine of Lynch's major works' (2008: 180). But unlike the films that surround Sailor's (Nicolas Cage) snide homophobic insults in *Wild At Heart* or Ben's (Dean Stockwell) epicene pastiche act in *Blue Velvet*, the simple sexual landscape of *Dune* can't bear the weight of the Baron. If the intent was to show the boy like a piece of meat – no more than the little animal (a 'squood') that Paul Smith's Rabban crushes and sucks dry a few minutes prior – then we leave Giedi Prime feeling we ate it ourselves, complicit rather than bearing witness.

FOLDING SPACE

The journey towards Arrakis begins with an almost unobtrusive montage of the Atreides family heading out of Caladan. Apart from the happy pug on Paul's lap, the scene is made all the stranger by the framing – the family is shot from afar, side-on, with no mobility between them, their ship and bodies seemingly automated. This recalls Chion's observation that *Dune* is a 'film of frozen portraits, continually open to questioning'; his opening thought on a passage of the film's several familial portraits (2005: 76). This passage scene and its little pug fit this description perfectly – 'the immobility, the hovering in place of these portraits is striking' – and he points out they recall the court portraits of Diego Velázquez, especially *Las Meninas* (1656).

That famous painting is a dour and complex arena of gazes and views; a dog in the lower view is his obvious touchstone but this strange sequence in *Dune* is self-conscious in the same idiom. We look at looking. To punctuate the point, the ships leaving Caladan literally enter a huge ornate gilt frame cut into the side of an

The members of House Atreides travel in their frozen poses

enormous tubular ship (a 'Guild heighliner' in the universe's jargon). Roger Ebert reflected on this first major space sequence by saying 'the spaceships are so shabby, so lacking in detail or dimension that they look almost like those student films where plastic models are shot against a tablecloth' (Ebert 1985). To my mind, this misses the sheer audacity of the shot. The film knows what it looks like, and tells you precisely where you're supposed to look. It's art time.

At this point the Third Stage Guild Navigator folds space in what is probably the film's most visually jarring effect. A wobbly colour overlay. Blurry bubbles. Gelatinous rays. Todd McGowan bravely tries to put words to the immense gap between the signified event and our actual experience: 'When space folds, one experiences a kind of enjoyment that one cannot access without the special qualities of the spice, but the film reveals this enjoyment as nonsensical' (McGowan 2007: 84).

The gallery is open, and we prepare to fold space

The scene has a quiet charm but the liquid particles standing in for stars are a kind of anti-effect – as discontinuous as if the words 'SPACE IS FOLDING NOW' were flashing in large print across the screen. Optical effects producer Kit West told Naha significantly that '*Dune* is not a special effects picture per se' (1984: 139), and while that's truer of *Dune* than *Star Wars*, due to their stylisation and relatively diminished role in the story, *Dune* ends up hinging on special effects all the more because we suspend expectation, not belief.

As Julie Turnock outlined in her history of special effects before computer-generated imagery overtook production, *Dune*'s effects are more comparable to science fiction films made a decade or so earlier – a fatal flaw considering the culture of effects enjoyment (Turnock 2014: 222). We're here to have fun, but we're not sure if we are.[20]

JUDGING THE CHANGE

Once on Arrakis, everything shifts. Visually. Sonically. Temporally. Vivian Sobchack argues that it's a paradox; while the 'open space of the desert is meant to be threatening' it 'functions like a breath of fresh air – releasing us from the dark, hermetic, hot-house interiors and demanding clutter of the film's insistent and material erotics' (1987: 267). This is exacerbated by the use of the 'Prophecy' theme by Brian Eno, cutting through the bombast of Toto's main score with a soft, warming drone. In fact, *Dune* as a film never really tells us to fear the desert; thirst is mentioned but never shown, the sun is present but never threatening.

The first real taste of Lynchian doom in *Dune* is in a short prophecy given by Reverend Mother Ramallo, played by Silvana Mangano, renowned for performances in such films as *Bitter Rice* (Giuseppe De Santis, 1949), *Ulysses* (Mario Camerini, 1954) and *Death in Venice* (Luchino Visconti, 1971). Her short warning is greatly expanded in a cut version of the scene, and for a long time it was Ramallo – not Irulan – who opened the film, right up to the near-final seventh draft of the script. In the cut sequence, she sits on a smoking reclining couch, a recurrent Lynch motif.[21] The reason for this excision may not be a complex one to decipher: Mangano was married to Dino De

Laurentiis for almost forty years but they separated as *Dune* was being edited.

The arrival of the Atreides family on Arrakis also heralds Max Von Sydow's memorable turn as Doctor Kynes, the 'Judge of the Change' who welcomes them to the planet and takes them on a tour of the spice mining operation. The tour inside an 'Ornithoper' craft continues the stilted, ornate ambience by having the rear of the craft rendered in plush buttoned material, with brassy levers at their front – another room designed for looking into and around, like an elevator in a plush hotel. J. Hoberman's mixed review for the *Village Voice* rightly noted that 'the film's preferred metal is not chrome but brass, its surfaces are not streamlined and shiny but dull, tarnished and typically adorned with weathered Deco patterns' (1984: 67). Of all the scenes in *Dune*, this one shows Bob Ringwood's costume work at its best; he discusses in a DVD feature how he wanted both erotic and tribal qualities in the Stillsuits, moulding them out of rubber (Sanctuary, 2004). Here we see Von Sydow's dusty well-worn suit against the Atreides newcomers, a detail that submerges entire pages of the Herbert plot but loses nothing in the visual shorthand.

Max Von Sydow's Kynes explains spice mining

Von Sydow anchors this sequence, giving other characters room to express their shock and awe. When Paul smells his fingers after the spice miners are rescued, the screen flashes white, and spice is immediately given the pure associations – with pleasure, power, a drug-like rush. McGowan notes this is similar to Henry touching the radiator in *Eraserhead* (2007: 8), but the rush experienced by Becky Burnett (played by Amanda Seyfried) in *Twin Peaks: The Return*, tilting her head back in chemical ecstasy, is now by far a closer analogue.

But our time on Arrakis isn't always as dramatically potent – the crucial plot turn of the Harkonnen attack, enabled by the betrayal of Dean Stockwell's character Dr. Wellington Yueh, is where the film's lyrical tension changes into a more staccato pace. In a tumble of quick scenes, we see an attack on Paul, an attempt to shore up the defences, Yueh's betrayal, the death of the Duke, the gloating of the Harkonnen, and finally, the escape of Paul and his mother Jessica. Against all these dramatic developments are the clash and rush of armies, explosions outside and bursts of hallway gunfire. In an ordinary science fiction adventure, this sequence would be a crescendo of action – clear movements, exciting turns, dramatic reveals.

While much of the writing on *Dune* simply refers to the 'action scenes' as a collective, Chion's close analysis looks at this sequence and the final battle together, and finds them wanting, with the bluntest of statements 'Lynch lacks the skill to make pure action scenes' (Chion 2005: 74).

Paul plays it cool against the hunter-seeker

This isn't entirely true. A beautiful, short action scene involves Paul evading a perfectly menacing 'hunter-seeker' slow-moving bullet and saving the life of Shadout Mapes (Linda Hunt) at the beginning of the Harkonnen attack sequence, and is all the more exciting by being shot like an argument between people. It comes after Paul tastes spice from a box, as if it were a sugary treat, and then immediately enters a short dream, showing Feyd, a laughing Reverend Mother Mohiam and the dark, dripping water – dream elements that refer both backwards and forwards in Paul's experience. Afterwards, Lynch shows a different skill, distilling the complicated concept of the Mentats in a few seconds. Thufir Hawat receives defence reports through a mysterious flashing light and translates them for the rest of House Atreides. It is unexplained, and requires no explanation. So, on one hand, the film misuses the time it has – but on the other, it seems to cut vertically and horizontally through thick mythos elements with a deft hand.

Yet there is one action beat that undeniably reinforces Chion's gripe. A Sardaukar trooper in a huge black bodysuit waves a gun down a hallway and we see a counter-shot of an Atreides officer falling down – no special effect from the gun or other effect is added. He just *waves it around*. He turns to face Duncan Idaho (played by Richard Jordan), who in turn *waves his gun around* and then punctures the Sardaukar's facemask. This would be forgettable on its own, but it's the only close-quarter combat of a large-scale battle happening outside. Thousands of extras, multiple armies, months of planning, surely the peak of Raffaella and Lynch's difficulties – but the resulting scenes evoke nothing of the care and tension of the interpersonal exchanges. Only one shot – Gurney yelling 'Long live Duke Leto!' while holding the family pug and leading a charge – is framed convincingly enough to make sense of the outside chaos.

Gurney keeps the pug safe during the charge

Right in the middle of this sequence, the film's charismatic spark still flickers in the shape of Dr. Wellington Yueh. It's not any of his prior scenes – not the early ones with Paul, or even the tense sobriety of his revelation to the Duke – but his death scene that bursts with life. Stockwell's Yueh is stabbed by Dourif's Piter and falls knees-first, face blood red with tension, and bellows: 'You think you've defeated me? You think you don't know what I've gained, for my wife?' It's hard to imagine anybody but Yueh roaring this line out with his body's last breath – turning on the firehose of camp to drench the scene.

As Jessica is bound, gagged and taken to the Baron for some gloating, he looms over her as a floating threat and says he 'wants to spit once on your head, just some spittle on your face' before he does so. Olson notes that here 'we viscerally register Jessica's involuntary shudder of revulsion' (2008: 183). Almost immediately, Piter de Vries insinuates rape, saying 'I've thought of many pleasures with you; it's maybe better that you die in the innards of a worm'. Lynch's works have been subject to a great deal of scrutiny as their morbid and surreal sexual violence often teeters over – or even freefalls into – exploitation aesthetics. Tracey Biga's review of *Blue Velvet* succinctly points out that the sexual violence in that film exists merely as 'a decision to study the male', where even in a complex form, women are enigmatic images and men are allowed a psychological journey (1987: 48). As *Twin Peaks: The Return* aired in 2017, some commentary on the show's treatment of women and sexual violence challenged the critical orthodoxy that postmodern pastiche was enough to excuse whatever the show threw at us (Gallagher 2017).

Only a few minutes later, the viewer isn't sure how to read the gender politics of a scene where Paul and Jessica mount an escape from their Harkonnen captors, as they lie bound together in the back of the ship. The troops are about to rape Jessica when Paul uses 'the voice', the commanding power of the Bene Gesserit, against them. He orders them to remove her gag, and she uses her own 'voice' to set them upon each other. Martha Nochimson calls this 'one of the most successful scenes' partially because of its sound design which lends it a dramatic power (1997: 127). However, just like the spitting scene, Jessica is not allowed enough agency to control the moment; her attention is immediately turned to observing her son. The allusion to rape is done quickly, executed for kicks, and only to benefit Paul and punctuate *his* journey: as Sabine Sielke has argued, this is the 'rhetoric of rape' (2002: 1) where sexual violence is used as a plot device to add weight or meaning to things other than the reality of sexual violence itself. Part of the context for this scene is that the novel's treatment of gendered violence, sexual violence and incest are all different and even more intense than the film's, and especially so as the Harkonnen and Atreides families are explicitly connected. Yet the scene falls flat because it feels like an attempted compromise between an escape sequence and expressive drama, both of which are overwhelmed by the smirking silliness of the assault.

Only once it is over, and they regain control of the ship, does pathos return – and only then because they become preternaturally aware that back in the palace, the Duke has finally been killed. With the tooth broken, the gas expelled, Piter and the Duke dead, and the Baron gleeful at his lucky escape, *Dune* begins a long sequence of visual and narrative darkness, and its special formal qualities are signalled loud and clear.

DUNE'S SPIRAL STRUCTURE

Remembering that Michel Chion analysed *Dune* as having a 'circular' or 'spiralling' structure, as part of an effort to make a 'feature-length, non-linear narration', it is in the late stages of the film that we should be seeing the outer spiral arms and circular waves (2005: 65). Lynch's experimentation with narrative film form and cinema matter is more recognisable in *Lost Highway* and, especially, *Mulholland Drive* (2001), but in the last hour of *Dune*, there's the beginnings of a method yet to be perfected. Chion's inkling was to trust Lynch at his own words rather than treat them as a throwaway statement, and the proof is that 'the story is given from the start rather than being doled out progressively' (2005: 65). But with the benefit of time, and seeing later Lynch works in relation to, *Dune*'s spiral structure is flagged clearly.

This can be seen to begin with by contrasting the film to Herbert's book. In the novel, it is the first moments in a cave hiding with his mother that Paul's growing preternatural awareness is described for us wholesale. He experiences a vision – a 'waking dream' which multiplies and guides him to choices, in part of what will become the *Dune* universe's all-important 'Golden Path', the series of events that characters are attempting to cling to in order to avoid chaos and bloodshed. In the film, this complex, inverse Buddhism is swapped for a more Lynchian approach; a dream that looks both backwards to reveal the plot of the Navigator, and forward to Feyd and the eventual birth of Alia. A lyrical punctuation is a hand, floating against the passing dunes, with a flapping flag overlaid.

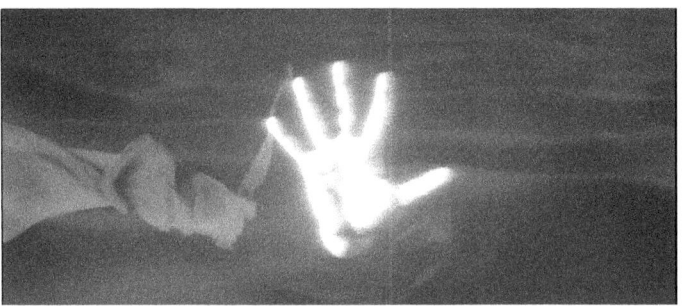

Loose dream images collide against the structural 'trailer' images

The first of four dream sequences occur as Jessica and Reverend Mother Mohiam argue in the opening moments on Caladan, meant to put the 'spectator in touch with the protagonist's extra-narrative energies' (Nochimson 1997: 130). What's at stake is an attempt to not just condense but refract the immense plot structure of the book into something visual, but to characterise Paul as he is in the book, feeling himself disassembling into possibilities, like a sand dune, or a dream. The second dream occurs immediately before the hunter-seeker assassination attempt, and serves mostly to signal that Paul is concerned about what the spice is doing to him. Paul's third dream, his 'waking dream', is perhaps the most significant, because he's able to relate it directly to his mother and bring the dream to life verbally.

Olson describes these sequences as lacking something; 'we just don't get the usual Lynchian feeling of actually experiencing deep human and cosmic mysteries, hypnotically floating into precincts that are terrifying and wondrous all at once' (2008: 186). Yet once understood in Chion's scheme as elements of an actual, concrete visual system – a circular map or spiral – they can be understood as much more than mysterious interludes. Although not all critics of *Dune* agree, Chion argues the dreams act like an anti-cinematic device, evoking 'the structure of trailers' (Chion 2006: 65).

So, the first dream is in Chion's language effectively a 'trailer' for the rest of the film; the second looks both forward and backward, the third concentrates on the unseen present. Paul doesn't dip in and out of a vast unconscious as much as in and out of the film's running order. The dreams give the character of Paul Atreides access to the film of *Dune*. He begins the dream with a thought ('Where are my feelings? I feel for no-one'). This signals that these sequences aren't emotional dreamstuff; they're structures.[22]

Something else crucially important also happens here. Paul is openly cruel and dismissive to his mother at this point in the novel, and Lynch attempts to keep some of this tension by having Paul ramp up his anger towards her. Paul is becoming something more than human, and his dream in the novel is more like a lysergic computer being turned on for the first time. The film never hints at the book's final revelation that Paul will become a tyrant. A longer version of the scene was shot which shows more of this rage, but it is easy to imagine it being cut down to avoid awkwardness in later scenes. But this is Francesca Annis's most interesting moment; with no spoken dialogue, we only have a few fragments of Jessica's inner voice. Held within her frightened but proud face is everything we need to carry the depth and weight of the scene in the book if we know it, and a taste of the events to come in the film if we don't.

Jessica realises what Paul is becoming and tries to hide it

After a worm chases Paul and Jessica across a patch of sand, they come across a Fremen group led by Stilgar (another soon-to-be Lynch regular, Everett McGill). No analysis of this sequence can avoid the fact that it is almost breaks the film's premise. Supposedly fearsome desert warriors, the Fremen fall almost instantly into line once Jessica grabs Stilgar's throat. The foreshortened part of this relationship implies that we're supposed to feel a 'measure of their faith in his potentially messianic nature' (Olson 2008: 184). Chion also singles out this scene, noting that 'the stately Fremen look like a troop of extras hired on the spot, clustering in front of the camera with big smiles. Their entrance makes for the only passage in *Dune* which is downright bad' (2005: 74). McGill's performance gives Stilgar a settled and stony-faced authority, but his introduction is so strangely constructed that it's difficult to define his relationship to Paul throughout the rest of the film.

PLANET ELLIPSIS

In the following sequence, *Dune* enters a kind of ellipsis effect. Scenes follow Paul and Jessica with the Fremen, but it could also be that chunks of time are passing with each scene. Some of the film's most striking images sit in this strange passage – for example, illustrator Paul Miller's preparatory paintings for *Dune* were nowhere better represented than in a scene at a water cache. In the bottom half of the frame, a huge watery blackness, barely perceptible – and above, long coruscating lines cut into the rock.[23] This deep stone blue against a clear black restores the film's visual language after a long sequence of blurred matte composites. The colouration of the Arrakis interiors seem to change over time, which is purposeful in the Arakeen palace and the Fremen sietch (village/meeting) areas especially. Production designer Tony Masters noted that the 'palace is red and blue but the sietches are green and black. The color of the sietches changes the deeper you go' (Naha 1984: 54-55). This gives the film a journey through colour and texture, coming to a rest deep underground in this reflective pool – our last real moment of peace in *Dune*'s running time.

Two scenes in this section of the film return to Giedi Prime, although even admirers of the film could be forgiven for feeling confused as to where characters are located by this stage. In a shower/steam room, the Baron gloats by flying around the room and bellowing while Nefud cranks a strange device and looks on. Paul Smith's Rabban saunters in, rips a tongue out from a hanging dead cow and celebrates with the Baron with some good old-fashioned cartoonish villain boasting – he's off to crush Arrakis and squeeze it for extra spice. Smith recalled this scene in the documentary, *Paul Smith: The Reddest Herring* (Har'el, 2008): from his perspective, it was a happy, professional environment that just happened to involve a frozen dead cow. He was even asked how he'd like the tongue to be cooked (he opted for sweet and sour).

When Jessica transmutes the blue 'water of life' successfully but in deep agony, she does so in an elegantly strange ceremony against even greener stone. A scene that showcased yet more interesting set design and prop elements was cut from this sequence, one showing the drowning of a young sandworm in order to produce the blue bile. We're additionally disoriented by Irulan's voice returning, explaining something we can see for ourselves; Reverend Mother Ramallo dies as Jessica survives. A later scene expands these blue-green environments even further, where Paul trains the Fremen how to use the 'weirding way' and to shatter stone with the spoken word. This scene recalls the purpose and energy of the film's earlier parts: it's almost as meticulously lit, staged and performed, much like the scene of Paul's training against the brass colossus on Caladan. As Paul was once trained, he now trains others – perhaps where the arms of the spiral swing past the same point on the radius. This training scene is where *Dune*'s ancient, ossified alternative brand of science fiction works the clearest – here, crucially, technology is as human as it is scientific. Paul's mantra-like statements drive the dialogue, his inner voice revelation – 'My name is a killing word' – is all we need.

After this manic, boisterous moment, we turn to Feyd. *Lovely Feyd*. Here comes Sting, emerging from the steam, glistening and lean, enjoying his uncle's lilting, amorous glances. This iconic shot revels in the singer's physique and would feature heavily in the film's promotion in Europe, where Sting's fame was a major drawcard.

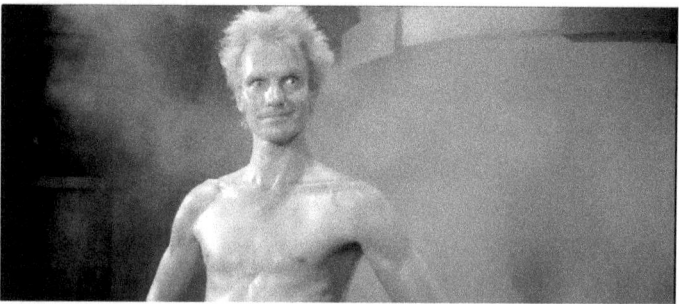

Feyd. Lovely Feyd

Godwin's diary includes the recording of a freeform, rambling exchange between Sting and co-star Sean Young that provides compelling insight into both actors. Sting mentions almost nothing about his music career in this exchange, and reveals instead that he has acquired rights to produce Mervyn Peake's novel *Gormanghast* (1950) with the intent to play Steerpike, which he would do in a 1984 radio adaptation alongside fellow Dune actor Freddie Jones (Godwin 2006: 341). Sting's sparkling, combative exchanges with Young reveal the delight he takes in playing a villain, and his most memorable scene is where he presents the tortured Thufir with a captured cat he must milk for the antidote to a poison – a Lynch trope, in keeping with the director's fascination with animal mutilation.

TOTAL AND PERMANENT MONTAGE

Dune's final stanzas can perhaps best be understood – evoking the idiom of science fiction – as accelerating to light speed. Emphasising Chion's description of the last part of *Dune* as 'total and permanent montage' (2005: 65) and recalling his claim for the film as 'feature-length, non-linear narration' that front-loads all its plot information, the last sequences of the film have to be treated as if they contained a different kind of plot, narration and structure. Across critical writing on *Dune*, there's vastly more written about the first ten minutes than the last thirty, the byproduct of this spiral structure that becomes feverish, wild and unrestrained.

Paul prepares to conquer Shai-Hulud

Paul gives a stirring speech to war to the Fremen inside the Hall of Rites – a stunning deep chasm filled with extras and rich matte effect work by Albert Whitlock. He trains the Fremen in the use of the weirding module, one of Lynch's additions to the *Dune* mythos that hints at 'tissue pulverization and spontaneous combustion' in description and gives an extravagant theatricality to the build-up to the major battle (Olson 2008: 169.) Paul's mantra returns – 'My name is a killing word' – speaking his inner voice while we imagine what's to come. Paul's declaration to the Fremen is absolute; their goal is to destroy not only the Harkonnen, but all spice mining – the complete collapse of the universal order.

When we hit a beautifully bright orange and brown desert shot of Paul heading towards the camera ready to ride the sandworm, we can almost smell the cinnamon air after nearly an hour of film without an extended sequence of brightly-lit environments.[25] The sandworms of Arrakis are meant to provide the terror and the delight at the heart of the mythos, in that they both produce and guard the spice. They were to have been the film's signature and most spectacular visual effect. Yet whatever imperfect fusion of science fiction effect and art film oddity the crew had imagined for them, nearly all the worm action sequences feel like staccato set-pieces. The optical compositing of Carlo Rambaldi's creations never quite elevates them to an actual menace. Sometimes they're not even visually distinct; as with many scenes, the foregrounds simply appear to be lit in a different hue than the backgrounds. Julie Turnock's observation that the optical printing was a bigger problem than the special effects themselves is nowhere truer than when Paul and Stilgar ride this giant worm together, harshly lit, dropped in against a distant background (2012: 140). Rather than triumphant warriors, they look like they're cruising for a party in an open-top car.

By the time the worm scenes were shot, cinematographer Freddie Francis had already left production. These were the only sequences he was not present for, as he believed they could be done without him and he had become deeply disillusioned with the production more generally (Francis 2013: 202). Although we don't seen them in the final film, Rambaldi innovated several new control techniques to get the worms to undulate and wriggle in visually interesting ways, the largest involving eighteen people behind the scenes. When asked how the worms were brought to life, Rambaldi answered wryly 'very carefully'(Naha 1984: 240).

As Paul and Stilgar are shown destroying spice harvesters (the same vehicle his father was so careful to evacuate) and carryalls (the flying wedge-shape craft that take the harvesters down to the sand) Irulan's voiceover returns: 'In the two standard years that followed, Muad'dib and the Fremen brought spice production to a standstill.' What follows is a rapidly overlaid montage – a composite montage of exploding ships, the Baron's bulbous nephew Rabban grimacing as his plans for domination crumble, rushing troops, the reveal of a young Alia, Paul and Chani kissing, Gurney Halleck being found on the battlefield and embracing Paul. This all occurs within the space of a single minute.

The clearest explanation of *Dune*'s last thirty-five minutes is best given by focussing on a scene that's in fact twenty-five minutes before the end – Paul taking the 'water of life'. We're told that if Paul survives the trial in the same way his mother did, he'll gain powers that will save the new, united Fremen front against the Harkonnen and the Emperor. Paul and Chani go to the desert during what appears to be night-time. Paul sips a blue liquid from a vial. The dream that should anchor us to Paul's journey doesn't seem to work like the others; we see water, worms, an eye, a hand, the Navigator. While the other three dreams moved up and down the structure of the film, here instead, his scattered inner voice tells us what we need to know – he controls the spice and the worms. What does occur is signalled to be a simultaneous event; Alia, Jessica and the Reverend Mother Mohiam bleed from their faces in response to Paul's awakening. During this dream, the two musical languages of *Dune* – Toto and Brian Eno – fade into each other and out again. Remembering that Lynch's 'ideal cinema' on the back of fixing and editing *Dune* for a year had 'dialogue coming in like music and sitting within a bed of sound effects', it's as if we can see in the construction of this sequence the birth pangs of Lynch's ideal cinema – the science fiction of his personal ambition (Lewis 1985: 8). The film's editor, Antony Gibbs, can only be the subject of endless sympathy given such a task – removing plotlines, shortening running time, combining ideas, finding options, footage returning with poor optical effects.

But that is not all this sequence does. Raffaella De Laurentiis explains in the introduction to the deleted material on the 2006 Universal Extended Edition DVD that the rumours of a super-long cut of *Dune* began with the 'assembly' cut of the film – missing effects shots and optical layering – made after principal photography. Coming in at four hours and twenty minutes, its size worried Universal, precipitating the pressure to hit a more conventional running time. Raffaella explained that the crucial scene of Paul taking 'the water of life' and finally becoming the Kwisatch Haderach was designed to replace six or seven deleted scenes (Universal 2006). Dino himself takes personal responsibility for pressuring Raffaella and Lynch; in Adrian Sibley's film *Dino De Laurentiis: The Last Movie Mogul* (2001), he laments that they 'had a fantastic movie when we did our cut' and that it was a 'mistake to listen to Universal'.

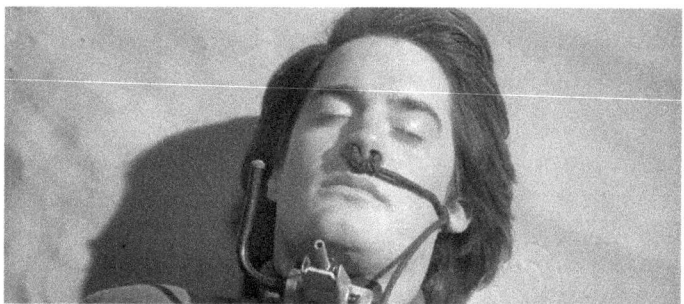

Paul transmutes the water of life; Lynch transmutes the film

This particular scene is where the scalpel cuts into the flesh. If the other dream sequences merely looked forward and backward through the film, this one does a lot more from a historical point of view – it looks up and down to the different versions of *Dune* that could have been: the *Dune* that was filmed; the *Dune* that Herbert fans yearned for; the *Dune* that inspired Lynch to focus forevermore on his ideal cinema. In the finished film, this sequence anchors the final 'act' – though Raffaella refers to it in that same DVD introduction as 'the film's epiphany' (Universal, 2006).

THE FINAL BATTLE

If *Dune*'s final battle is meant to be its epiphany, it is a slow and deliberate one. The action sequences – armies and ships shooting, things exploding – are set up in a dreamlike, disconnected atmosphere. The circular/spiral structure that leads us here feels more like a brush dipped in ink and then drawn in a continuous motion until the brush runs dry. *Dune* concludes first with a whimper, then an almighty bang. Baron Harkonnen and Nefud are summoned to Arrakis to deal with Rabban's failure to stop the mysterious Muad'dib. The Emperor comes down in a golden ship, after a brief threat from the Guild to take care of things personally. Paul marshals the Fremen for full-scale war. All these events could be happening over a lengthy period of time or a single night. In a regular science fiction adventure, we'd have no doubt of the course of events leading up to this battle.

Some shots required the entire De Laurentiis movie making apparatus and experience to organise, with thousands of extras rushing from caves, an impressive flow of human life, requiring weeks of organisation and work and doubtlessly huge chunks of the budget – but not a single shot in the battle sequences is given the time to resonate or given enough partial configuration to become dramatic in the sense expected of screen science fiction. It's also here that the dramatic cuts to the effects budget and plan bite hardest. Rambaldi's creature shop was working with a bigger effects list before the cuts came in; as he told Naha, the sixteen worms he built would eventually 'look like thousands of worms' (1984: 239). But this does not appear in the final film, although it is hinted at by Ron Miller's rich production paintings lovingly curated at the website Duneinfo.com. where a colourful deluge of gigantic worms appears to rush the Emperor's redoubt.

When Paul, Stilgar and Gurney prepare an atomic attack and ride the worms through the miniature wreckage, it represents months of work by dozens of people, through perhaps hundreds of pre-production and production iterations – but we're more interested to see inside the gleaming golden Lighter where the Emperor is being tormented by young Alia with the revelation that Paul is Muad'dib. Outside, the optical effects are distracting and distancing – but back indoors is where all of *Dune*'s power is churning away. The worm-riders shunt blasts of energy into the sand, flattening Sardaukar troops, but we can't wait to go back inside and re-establish contact with the dramatis personae.

After Alia disposes with the Baron with a slice of her 'gom jabbar' (the same poisoned needle that held Paul helpless while being tested by the Reverend Mother's box), he spins out of an imploded wall and into the mouth of a worm. For him, an ignoble end comically rendered, for Alia, a lasting resolution, poetically drawn. She is suddenly swept outside and revels in the chaos and bloodshed – a simple slow-motion shot that hints at her wider role in the *Dune* universe of the novels as an eventual tyrant. All of *Dune*'s capacity for richly woven euphoric drama and the loose threads of its visual language are evident in a single moment. It's the last inward breath before the final scene.

Alia revels in death, hints of her character in the novels

A beat of silence, a multi-coloured staircase inside the Arrakeen palace. *Dune*'s final scene opens with militaristic machismo and rows of arrayed characters and extras awaiting the final pronouncements, as if in a courtroom – what Chion referred to as 'affected pictorialism' (2005: 83). Paul, Gurney, Stilgar and the new-look full Bene Gesserit Jessica saunter with some Fremen into a room already filled with them – row upon row of stillsuits fill the space, with a few captured Sardaukar.[26] Into the room are marched Feyd, Nefud, the Emperor, Irulan and many minor military figures the film never had time to name. Outside waits the throng of victorious Fremen. Olson compares this scene to Edward Hicks's painting *The Peaceable Kingdom* (circa 1833), in which humans and animals are arrayed together in cloying romance (2008: 175). But this is the return of *Dune*'s rich interior power, not just a depiction of Paul's authority over a collective scene.

The final battle begins with words. Paul bends the Reverend Mother, and by extension the Emperor, to his will by yelling 'silence'. The Fremen show their religious fealty to Paul by warning those in the room not to stand against the 'righteous'. This word sets off Feyd, who demands a duel. A few swerves and curves, a remembered lesson from Gurney, and Feyd is thrown to the ground and stabbed (Sting's undeserved reputation for a poor performance in the film likely arises from this fight). Paul rises and *yells* Feyd's body into the stone, and we're told that 'Usul no longer needs the weirding module' by one of the Fremen Fedaykin. As it began with the voice, it ends with the voice.

Paul's dominance over the universe is almost complete. A great deal was cut from this sequence, notably the death of Thufir Hawat and a deeply troubling set of pronouncements by Paul (including the declaration of Irulan as his wife and Chani as his concubine). While these cuts were painful for Herbert fans, the ethical framework of the film would have been far worse – women far closer to chattel, and the tragedy of lost friends more wasteful. Poor Thufir, disappearing from his position in the courtly arrangement from one shot to the next, is presumably left alive. Irulan's final narration begins with a now full-throated religious conviction – 'Muad'dib has become the hand of God' – and it ends as we cut to a shot that includes her standing by her father's side. Paul accepts the mantle of Godhood fully with more mantras – 'God created Arrakis to train the faithful; one cannot go against the word of God' – and opens his mouth to exhale in an extremely subtle final act, triggering rainfall on Arrakis amidst a final flurry of dreamscape oceans and blue-within-blue eyes. Alia has the last word, confirming what the film has told us – Paul *is* the Kwisatch Haderach.

Both Frank Herbert and Harlon Ellison stress the relative weakness of the film's ending; a cascade of magical rain on the desert planet instead of the more complex resolution that Paul is a boy playing at being a God, and mostly getting away with it.[27] The film's ending is *too* final, *too* complete as a result. Yet although the film rushes towards this conclusion, its final moments are carved from stone and spoken like an ancient ritual. The spiralling structure has finally come to rest somewhere familiar; a mantra spoken to end a quarrel. Paul's final breath and Alia's confirmation give the film what is best described – with respect to Toto's soundtrack – as a prog-rock ending. It's tempting to make a link to Jeffrey Beaumont's ending in *Blue Velvet* – a saccharin excess where 'culture and energy are revealed in balance' (Nochimson 1997: 122), but Paul's cooling breath isn't balance, it's an annihilation.

Yet earlier in Lynch's script stages, *Dune* ended very differently. In the second draft, we travel inside Paul's blue eye – 'suddenly appearing in the blue light is the blood ocean of the jihad, its waves rolling like red glass into the future'. In the fifth draft, it was a more calming 'ocean of light rolling like gold glass off into the infinite'. In the seventh, a final image seemed to take Lynch's fantasy into a direction closer to his personal belief system of Transcendental Meditation and the enduring legacy of the Maharishi – something that would have made *Dune* a more personal film. In that version, after the gold glass, 'the blue becomes darker and a golden lotus flower blooms in the night'. Had the film ended on a blooming flower set against a blue field, it would have matched the very first frame after the credits in *Blue Velvet* – roses against the blue sky. Just as *Elephant Man* and *Dune* were connected visually in some hidden personal system, so would have more Lynchian *Dune* straddled time and space to better match the film that would give him back the auteur authority and control he craved – *Blue Velvet*.

McGowan's extended critical reading of *Dune* analyses the released film's ending with a unique twist. He begins with a similar framing of many of the director's critics: that David Lynch is not Hollywood, that Dune was too Hollywood, and for David Lynch to be good, *Dune* must die the little death (McGowan 2007: 69). McGowan identifies that at the film's conclusion, we have an 'enjoyment completely opposed to pleasure' because we 'see the consequences of our fantasy' (2007: 71-72). This is no small observation; it's a rare close reading of the film that takes it on its own terms – as a Lynch film but also, not. One that positions Paul as a tragic victor but equally, makes the order of the film's universe as tragically interwoven with him. It's a satisfaction, but the satisfaction of relief as much as exultation.[28]

The first shot of Blue Velvet *after the credits; a flower in the blue sky*

Dune's ending reinforces the sense that the film is not some arcane puzzle to be solved, rich with hidden meanings waiting for the right key. Rather, it has textures, sensual pleasures, intense stand-offs, powerful mantras, a self-serious tone and a lingering affective landscape that has no equal anywhere in film science fiction.

Footnotes

15. Greg Olson expands the analysis to other Lynch figures, calling the trope 'The Woman Who Floats in Space', also connecting Irulan to *Industrial Symphony Number One*, *Wild at Heart* and *Twin Peaks: Fire Walk With Me* (Olson 2008: 161).
16. While many rooms have elements of this complex honeycombing effect, the Abencerrajes room and courtyard is rumoured to be the site of a great plot and betrayal between two rival families – where the Abencerrajes wiped out the Zegris.
17. It was also the sequence of one of the film's more serious on-set accidents; at some point in the preceding days, the Navigator tank had completely crushed the foot of a mechanical effects assistant (Naha 1984: 256).
18. Lynch is clear about how he uses and reuses themes and images across his work; he has fascinations which inspire him and he comes back to concepts in new ways. Throughout *Twin Peaks: The Return*, more *Dune* reference points are there if you go looking. A cracking egg appears in a dream. A spindly horror-creature with bent arms spits out spheres in a gelatinous ray. Only the most obvious references are highlighted in this chapter.
19. To my mind, this immense set-piece is a clear inspiration point for the interior of the Borg Cube in *Star Trek: The Next Generation*'s second season episode 'Q Who' – along with the green-light grids, pipe-headed black-clad antagonists which draw on the Harkonnen, Guildsmen and Sardaukar for various visual flourishes.
20. Turnock's historical analysis is borne out by the differences in the different Lynch script versions as they hemmed in over the months and years. At one early point in the script's development, the Guild Navigator brings a shining triangle of light towards a large group of other Navigators, who chant and manipulate a miniature universe. This shift is one of the many that took place as the scope of the effects was reduced, in the wake of Raffaella's decision to oversee them directly.
21. This can be seen most famously with Sheryl Lee's Laura Palmer smoking as she writes in her diary in *Twin Peaks: Fire Walk with Me* and in *Wild at Heart* when Laura Dern's Lula smokes in bed and delivers that film's eponymous line, 'This whole world's wild at heart and weird on top'.
22. Martha Nochimson noted that these scenes are meant to decentre the deeply masculine fantasies of *Dune*, as Paul's relationship with women is rendered 'with more fluidity and interest' than with men (Nochimson 1997: 130). Olson supposes that in both the novel and the film, 'Paul Atreides emerged as an archetype of positive integration: a "masculine"

warrior and leader who relies on his "feminine" intuition and the wisdom of the sisterhood' (Olson 2008: 152). These two analyses aren't incompatible; in the novel's mythos, Paul is integrated into a feminine order whose primary function is to see through time and space.
23. Miller's painting is nearly completely translated inch by inch for the environment (even more screen time with it survives in the Alan Smithee version).
24. Lynch famously had a long-running art project involving dismembered animals and displaying their parts like a science project with absurd captions. During the making of *Dune*, he made a 'Chicken Kit' and a 'Duck Kit', the latter of which didn't photograph to his satisfaction – which was probably no consolation to the duck (Olson 2008: 501-502; Breslin 1997: 80).
25. In the worm-riding scene, Stilgar's Fremen have red shoulders. We're shown them being painted as such to become the Fedaykin, Paul's assault troops and bodyguards – but in the next scene. It's a minor continuity error in some respects, but as this scene precedes a vast jump in time, it's doubly disorienting.
26. Special note should be made of the character Harah, given prominent place in the room as she seemingly waits Paul's arrival. She was the wife of Jamis, the Fremen that Paul kills in a deleted scene. She and her two children, one holding a squirming pug, are squarely placed in the centre of the establishing shot. Since their entire plotline was excised in the editing phase, their presence here is like a ghost of a version of the film long since murdered.
27. Even though the film ends with god-given rainfall, Herbert fans sometimes point to the *muted* religiosity of the film's overall plot; Paul's visions are not of humanity's collective future, and we don't ever hear much about the fictive premise of genetic memories, of the Bene Gesserit implanting the Messiah myths among the Fremen, and so on.
28. The ending of the film is also structurally and thematically troublesome for some Herbert fans. It alters the events of the later books and contains many contradictions not obvious or important to the film viewer.

4. THE SLEEPER HAS AWAKENED: AFTER *DUNE*

As principal photography ended, and the tortured editing process and the lengthy special effects manufacturing began, anxieties were building about the film's reception. In a dark augury of the waiting world, Naha notes that 'During the last days of shooting a wrap party is held at a nearby arena wherein cast and crewmembers are invited to step into a bullring and "fight" baby bulls' (1984: 256). It's hard to imagine a more dark and loaded celebration that tousling with unwilling animals, but like so many of the anecdotes during production, the clarity only comes in retrospect. The picture painted across all the sources, interviews, diaries and re-assessments of *Dune* is that this was a kind of science fiction film-making about to meet its end. The movie-making enterprise that the De Laurentiis family specialised in – the old-fashioned hardscrabble yardwork which had produced decades of success – was already giving way to specialist teams, massively reduced choices in special effects production pipelines, and a blockbuster system rapidly swallowing up larger chunks of the distribution system. No more wrestling with bulls; more anodyne and safer sports were on their way.

Part of the reason that *Dune* arrived with a feverish shock, and that reviewing critics were often bamboozled, is that they were both arguably primed to see it fail by the advance press, and then unwilling to credit its vertical walls of strangeness. Here was simultaneously a science fiction film they could openly punish, and an art-house darling they could admonish. Dennis Lim summarises the critical reception well, by saying that the 'tone of the advance press was ominous' and that the press loved 'a costly folly' (Lim 2015: 63).

Ominous was right; stories that hundreds of men scoured the desert to rid it of rattlesnakes, scorpions and debris led the film's pre-release coverage in *The New York Times* and elsewhere – and the clamour was verging on hysterical. But not everyone was drunk on *schadenfreude*: it would be remiss not to mention Tom O'Hanlon gushing about the possibility of a billion-dollar *Dune* franchise equal to the Disney empire itself (1984: 70). Lynch, to his credit and despite his misgivings and the ordeal of production, was on the hustings fighting negative rumours where he could.

Perhaps it was more than mere gossip-mongering that he was up against. It seems to be undeniable that Universal and others indulged in a bit of myth-making, happily sharing information about on-set trouble and disasters as part of the build-up to release. The Naha book, as an officially licensed product, must have passed through several editorial passes – none of which saw fit to remove the eye-watering production problems, exasperated crew, or stories of Mexican locals being chased away from the sets. All this lent credence to the sense that Universal didn't know how to market such a difficult film. But in retrospect, maybe it's more true to say that *Dune*'s trouble *was* the product for sale.

Viewed through this slightly conspiratorial lens, a lot of otherwise unremarkable elements suddenly become glaring. For example, Hoyts Distribution in Australia released production notes to the film as part of its press kit – presumably drawn from long-forgotten Universal marketing materials. The press kit quotes Lynch at length:

> There was one dog dead at the top of the dump, and we walked down amongst those strange rocks and there was a dead pig that had a huge slash – dead. Lots of dead dogs, a dead rat. (Lynch, quoted in Hoyts: 1984)

The reputation of Las Aguilas Rojas, nicknamed as the 'dead dog dump', is explained even more luridly here than in Godwin's nihilistic diary entries of the days being there and seeing the mess of corpses for himself. Were the press supposed to go into the film with anything other than concern after reading anecdotes like this? This was myth-making at its most paradoxical: see how hard we worked! The conditions we were under! The sacrifices we've made! But the picture painted in this press kit is more than that, as it invites critics and journalists to take some perverse pleasure in the debacle. The audience, with their glossary sheets that outlined key terms for the film before they went in (discussed further below), got two pages of homework. With press kits like this, critics had their homework done for them.

So abundant were negative reviews that indexing them (let alone comprehensively covering them) would be an arduous task. But some offered more balanced perspectives of what audiences should be prepared for: Paul Attanasio for *The Washington Post* said it had 'staggering visual power' but was also 'stupefyingly dull and disorderly' (1984: C1); J. Hoberman famously called his piece for *The Village*

Voice 'The End of Science Fiction' but was taken by the film's 'ancient primordial nastiness that has nothing to do with the sci-fi film as we currently know it' (1984: 68). Pauline Kael's review in *The New Yorker* famously said that Lynch 'doesn't conquer this Goliath – he submits to it'. For Kael, Lynch 'lacks vulgar show-biz talents', but also intriguingly mentions that Paul takes Irulan as a wife at the film's conclusion (1984: 78). This was ultimately taken out of the final cut, meaning that some critics at least were seeing a version still undergoing changes, and not the version audiences saw in cinemas.

Elsewhere, more positive voices warmed to the film: John Baxter in *Vogue* wrote that the film contains 'fugitive visual delights; science fiction literally down to earth in both its plot and tones of rust, cinnabar and ochre' (1984: 89). A positive review by legendary Australian critic Bill Collins asks viewers to 'enjoy the sensuous experience' in a later piece when the film was released for the home video market (1985: n.p.). David Ansen, film critic for *Newsweek* at the time, appeared on a 2004 DVD extra feature called 'Impressions of *Dune*' in which he repeats the charge that other critics developed a groupthink negativity, and that they refused to give it any credit for its difference and inventiveness (Sanctuary, 2004). Ansen deserves special mention in this interview for suggesting that *Dune* had 'not yet come in for a major reassessment', that it was 'overdue for a rediscovery', and that 'maybe some years down the way they'll realise it's a much stranger and more interesting movie' than critics said it was on release. As we saw in Chapter Two, it remains important for many critics and academics loyal to Lynch's self-created authorial brand to treat *Dune* not just as aberrant but absent.

This rediscovery, if it has begun at all since Ansen's interview in 2004, belongs to the cadre of *Dune* loyalists on social media and fragmentary articles which ask people to search their memories for their own reassessment. For example, the film's cult status as a '*Star Wars* for Goths' (DeVore 2017) cutely sums up all the film's tenacious weirdness and enduring appeal. DeVore argues that it attracts a certain type of person *already* alienated by science fiction's mainstays, and in so doing, perhaps becomes an art-house cinema for nerds – a gateway drug for those heavily invested in science fiction but with a developing taste for more experimental fare. In 1986 Raffaella De Laurentiis believed that they had been too faithful to the book, and said getting out from the shadow of *Star Wars* proved too difficult, that they were 'pretentious enough to think we could do it a different way' (Friendly 1986). That pretension is exactly why the film's tenacious fandom and reputation has held together; a pure enjoyment of the different way.

To tell the story of *Dune*'s cultural impact in this chapter, I'll consider the actual box office numbers to assess the damage of the so-called bomb. I then revisit some of the strange collection of the merchandise and examine the series of videogames which significantly contributed to the film's enduring cultural legacy, but which all too often fall under the radar of screen media scholars. Finally, I look back at *Dune* with the benefit of hindsight, to consider its legacy and meaning for contemporary audiences today.

THEY TRIED AND DIED

For all the stories of *Dune*'s box office failure, the conditions by which it failed with audiences seemed obscure and abstract. Dr. Dean Brandum, a film historian and film exhibition scholar, used *Variety*'s 'Top Fifty' data set, which covers twenty key cities/territories which historically represent 35 per cent of the US box office income, to produce for this book an in-depth analysis of *Dune*'s box office.[29] Importantly, Brandum found the weak point in the domestic US release was the crucial third week, ending on the 2 January 1985. This was a time movie-goers traditionally had more money and time and were out in large groups. Rather than gaining 45 per cent per screen average gross in this week like the average of the top twenty films represented in the selected cities at the time, *Dune* picked up only 9 per cent (Brandum, personal communication 2018). Brandum suggests that the exhibitors that had the film booked must have smelled blood in the water and immediately realised that the screen would be better used picking up more screenings of *Beverly Hills Cop* (Martin Brest, 1984) or taking a chance on a new release. *Dune* also faced direct competition from other science fiction films such as *Starman* (John Carpenter, 1984) and *2010* (Peter Hyams, 1984). While both *2010* and *Dune* fared poorly, the former still drew in bigger audiences during that crucial third week. Brandum suggests that there are usually only a certain number of genre fans who will see concurrent films, exacerbating their competition during a critical period. A more 'general audience' was very likely to be seeing *Beverly Hills Cop*, other comedies, or – heading into Oscar season – prestige titles like *Amadeus* (Miloš Forman, 1984) and *The Killing Fields* (Roland Joffé, 1984).

Brandum adds that a film of *Dune*'s size and budget is usually relaunched in cheaper cinemas to give them a longer life, but in this case – for reasons that are unclear – it did not happen. Across these twenty key markets, *Dune* averaged around $4,000 dollars per screen it was shown on during its fourth, fifth, sixth, seventh and eighth week (Brandum, personal communication 2018). It then disappeared from cinemas completely. Whether there was a collective realisation of better options with other films, or whether Universal intervened, we may never know. And, perhaps, there was simply something in the weather: the month *Dune* was released was the coldest month in the US since 1899, with freezing temperatures recorded all the way down in Georgia (Burt 2014). Perhaps for some, the idea of spending more than two hours in the shimmering desert heat was too much. *Dune* was certainly not alone with its disappointing takings for its studio: Universal experienced a horror year in 1984 with only modest successes. It would not be until *Back to the Future* (Robert Zemeckis, 1985) that Universal would have their next major success, made for less than half the budget of *Dune*, but taking in $210 million compared to *Dune*'s $30 million.

As Frank Herbert notes in his introduction to *Eye*, however, there is an argument to be made against focusing solely on the US market – noting that screenings in France and the UK remained popular into the third week (Herbert 1985: 12). Many factors in isolation could explain such a discrepancy. *Dune*'s overseas posters foregrounded Sting, and the film entered a different science fiction landscape in France, where locally produced films *Le Dernier Combat / The Last Battle* (Luc Besson, 1983) and *Le Prix du Danger / The Prize of Peril* (Yves Boisset, 1983) had been in the theatrical mix. Even the artist Moebius's attempts to help make *Dune* could have been a factor, as by then many of his comics were famous in the Francosphere.

But Universal struggled to make *Dune* accessible. One of the most celebrated and historically curious aspects of the film's distribution is a '*Dune* Terminology' paper handout. These were handed out by ushers in at least six US cities, and more apocryphally, copied and translated overseas. In short, they were a double-sided glossary of key narrative terms printed on newspaper stock. Explaining terms like *Kwisatch Haderach*, *Sardaukar* and *Muad'dib* may have been a solvable problem, but many of the terms are plainly understandable in the context of the dialogue – such as the Baron spitting at Piter De Vries that 'the forms of *kanly* have been obeyed' after being told the good Duke Leto doesn't wish to speak or meet with him. We know immediately by insinuation that *kanly* must be some formal vendetta system; enough, at least, to move on. In fact, the sheet probably made things *more* confusing by introducing terms and ideas that go unreferenced in the film. While little information remains about how wide the distribution of this sheet was, it seems more likely that it contributed to the confusion surrounding the film's inescapably dense mythology, rather than neutralising it.

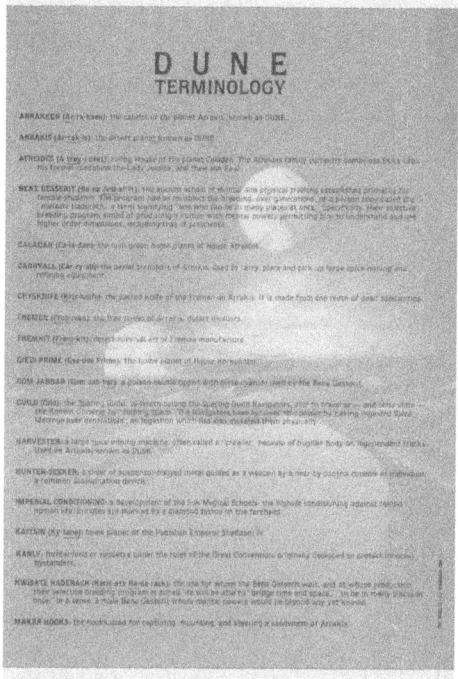

The famous 'Dune Terminology' handout (from the author's collection)

Whatever work the '*Dune* Terminology' handout was supposed to do, those who received it left the theatre with their first (and perhaps only) piece of *Dune* merchandise, precisely when the shadow of *Star Wars* was passing at last, and new adventures in space were expected.

THE HARVESTERS OF *DUNE*

A film's cult status is difficult to quantify, and perhaps also misleading. What's more valuable in *Dune*'s case is persistence. Looking at social media today, you could be forgiven for thinking that *Dune* was a major success as images of the production, tie-in children's books, toys and magazines are lovingly shared; these photos are much more common than actual stills from the film. In some cases, like the *Dune Pop-Up Panorama Book* or the colouring and activity books, there's a deep incongruity between the film we see and the market intended – there's something almost perverse about a dead Piter De Vries and Duke Leto to be coloured in, a maths puzzle to calculate the weight of the pustulant Baron. Whatever publisher Putnam wanted for these tie-ins, they must have been utterly dismayed at the film's short theatrical life in the United States. In 1984, O'Hanlon mentions a 'World of *Dune*' teaching kit that introduced themes and characters, distributed free to 4,000 junior high and high school teachers across the United States and Canada, and an attempt by Universal, Putnam and Berkley to create fan clubs 'where they don't exist' (1984: 70). There is no small irony that a film about undoing the deserts would be followed by a failed astroturfing campaign from a marketing perspective.

While these were examples of merchandising folly, others products bear the trace of a closer relationship with the production teams at Universal. For example, the Fleer Corporation released a set of *Dune* trading cards and stickers, sold in packets with a stick of chewing gum. Each featuring an early on-set photo or a still from an unfinished rush of a scene, they are representative of the style of film collectable cards that proliferated in card and hobby shops dominated by sports trading cards. Fleer's cards came in a cinnamon orange pack, with the edges of the photos similarly finished in a burnished red – tying in with *Dune*'s colour scheme. The most significant feature of these cards is that they were produced before the film's final cut, which resulted in the inclusion of several of the scenes from the Alan Smithee version (such as a fight with the doubting Fremen warrior Jamis – a crucial moment in the novel – Paul telling Chani she would be a concubine, and Thufir's death). It is also highly telling that of the 128 Fleer cards, the final sequence (which, as noted in the previous chapter, takes less than a quarter of the running time) is the subject of 45% of the cards. Whenever the Fleer cards were produced, it was clearly before the editing process had taken these scenes out of the final cut, and perhaps then it seemed the battles would be filled out more completely.

Joan D. Vinge's *The Dune Storybook* (1984) likewise tells the story of a *Dune* that was never made; paced differently, it has newly added scenes, and includes an even more complex telling of the 'water of life' sequence from the original script. Filled with sometimes dark photographs of the film's production, most notably the key effects sequences were not represented at all (these were obviously created after the book went into production). Similarly, the glossy making-of magazine *Dune Official Collector's Edition* by Paradise Press contains the same longer plot as *The Dune Storybook*, but also – just like *The Making of Dune* and the Australian press kit – bewilderingly includes a tremendous amount of negative anecdotes about the production of the film. To indicate how rushed this material appeared to be produced, this magazine came with a separate insert called *Dune Official Poster Magazine Edition* which fills the back of two posters of Kyle MacLachlan and Sting with the exact same copy from the magazine the pull-out itself appears in: again we have a repetition of an unnecessarily complex version of the plot, and more negative anecdotes. We can only conclude that many of these tie-ins were produced by licensees who were given a somewhat random, arcane and obtusely selected collection of material to work with. Simply put, Universal externalised its own doubts and worries about the film in its marketing machine. Some of these materials look like a film studio biting its nails and thinking out aloud.

Yet some of the tie-in products are impressive artefacts in their own right, such as the exceptional *Dune* comic. Produced by Marvel in 1984 as a single magazine, it was also released in a three-part regular comic format, and then in different forms thereafter. Scripted by Ralph Macchio (no relation to the *Karate Kid* actor) and drawn by legendary artist Bill Sienkiewicz, the *Dune* comic is astonishing in its pacing, tone

Examples of Dune *promotional merchandise (from the author's collection)*

and kinetic energy. Coloured in one set of tones for the original and then again for the lighter paperweight of individual comics, these were regular features of Marvel's movie tie-in line-up during the period (similar comics were released to coincide with other science fiction and adventure films), but few match the production quality and approach of *Dune*. Granted the autonomy to take faces and objects from the film where they worked, and to expand and improvise where they didn't, Sienkiewicz exploded the barriers of the film's effects and rendered Macchio's mostly faithful script with effortless clarity. There are many highlights: a desert image in the sequence where Liet Kynes tours the Atreides around the planet is rendered in incredible simplicity; the sandworm which devours the sandcrawler is rendered at shocking scale, with dark jagged lines. Elsewhere, lines from Herbert's original novel that never appeared in Lynch's are integrated with the film's visual language (again also drawing from the version of the story before the final cut). Sienkiewicz's jagged, languid style rendered all the dream sequences in florid, flowing arrangement far more successfully than the film itself: a single abstract page replaces the movie's clumsy montage sequences. The success of the comic provides further evidence that the 'inner voice' which so many blamed for *Dune*'s impenetrability was itself spawned potentially from these origins, Chion noting 'it is almost unique for an inner voice to be shared by a number of characters, though this convention is frequently found in comic strips' (2006: 66). While this element may not have worked in the film, in the *Dune* comic it fit like a glove. From this perspective, the Macchio/Sienkiewicz *Dune* comic is almost a post-production storyboard – rather than a sketch to build up a film, this is a sequence of the potential images taken to a satisfying conclusion that the film itself was sometimes unable to. A director's cut, just without the director, or the cut.

THE GAMES OF *DUNE*

For a few years following its initial release, Lynch's *Dune* was virtually forgotten, submerged almost completely into the sands of time. A few peripheral forms of genre media – notably strategy and roleplaying games – drew from its broader universe either through official licenses or by taking artistic liberties in re-adapting an aspect here and there. But soon after the financial collapse of Dino De Laurentiis's film empire in the wake of the film's considerable losses, the rights reverted to Universal. In 1990, Martin Alper of Virgin Games (a subsidiary of the Virgin Group corporation) finally acquired the rights to produce videogames and related media. Through this, *Dune* experienced a strange rebirth, although the games themselves had a long, unusual history of preproduction, hostile corporate takeovers and collapsing faith; this a saga well covered in Daniel Ichbiah's French-language game history book *La Saga des Jeux Vidéo* (*The Saga of Videogames*, 2017). This second wind is meaningful because it may explain how many people's relationship to the film has strengthened over time – they repeated not only images and ideas from the Lynch version but added to the mythos and narrative Universe far outside the official Herbert orthodoxy. It also happens that, by extension, *Dune* would become an important part of videogame design history.

The game that first emerged out of this agreement between Virgin, French videogame production team Cryo, and Universal was simply called *Dune* (1992). It used a picture of Kyle MacLachlan in his stillsuit on the retail box, video snippets of Irulan's opening speech and other visual elements, such as Jessica Atreides looking somewhat like Francesca Annis but not close enough to require the license they attained from MacLachlan to replicate his image. Ichbiah explains that the *Dune* licence allowed Cryo to use audio snippets from the film in a very early example of the expanded opportunities of CD-ROM game software, and a few other stylistic elements also drawn from Lynch's film (Ichbiah 2017).

This strategy game was available for Amiga, MS-DOS on PCs and the SEGA-CD system, and allowed players to develop an economy of spice as Paul as they convinced the Fremen to unite with him against the Harkonnen and eventually overwhelm the planet. Like many movie license games, it takes vast liberties with the source material, but the expanded time-frame of videogame play provide an opportunity to explore the *Dune* universe far more intricately than in the movie itself. The game returns to Lynch's version now and then for elements it needs to ground the slow-burn adventure, but it is strengthened significantly by the practical differences between the film and videogames – the battle against the Harkonnen is a slow, calculating affair and your option to begin undoing the desert by planting greenery is a deeply satisfying way to imagine the narrative of the film progressing.

That same year, Westwood Studios also released *Dune II: The Building of a Dynasty* for MS-DOS, Amiga and the SEGA Megadrive/Genesis, under a concurrent license for Virgin. That game borrowed much less from the film itself, and instead put players in control of one of three armies as an unnamed commander. Players built a base, which helped you fund an army, and then you defeated your enemy. The style of gameplay it established, although it had some predecessors, would famously become known as real-time gameplay – directly inspiring Westwood Studios' own *Command & Conquer* (1995) and Blizzard Entertainment's *Warcraft: Orcs and Humans* (1994) and is one of the most influential videogame designs of all time through these two series alone. It was very much the blockbuster success everybody associated with the film had wanted, but deferred, delayed and transported to another medium.

In *Dune II*, players would navigate the screen with a mouse/cursor and manage a vast system that looked more like the operating system of their computer. This novel gameplay experience allowed the game easy access, and its massive success meant more people being exposed to the *Dune* universe, now enduring and developing new audiences who otherwise might not be drawn to either the novels or the film. To emphasise this long relationship, 1998 would see Westwood re-release the game in an adapted format called *Dune 2000*, and then later, *Emperor: Battle for Dune* (2001). Renowned for their full-motion video inclusions in games for many years, Westwood opted to film scenes for the beginning of each mission. This time, the Lynch production – complete with Tony Masters's designs, Bob Ringwood's costumes and even some acting tics – is used as direct inspiration. From bushy Mentat eyebrows to the bald Bene Gesserit, dozens of visual elements were reconstructed.

Videogame studies have parsed games of this era in different ways, but most compelling is a more generally useful term – Mia Consalvo's use of the notion of 'paratexts'. Ordinarily thought of as a relationship between a main text and its peripheral objects (such as the way we might think of film's relationship to its marketing material), Consalvo challenges the ordering of importance between these texts and objects and argues that in the videogame media environment, texts exist in a more complex continuum (2009: 21). This is especially important in the case of instruction guides, booklets and videos which assist players who might otherwise be at a disadvantage. From this perspective, these scenes from *Dune 2000* which directly reference Lynch's film act like paratexts of the 1984 film. Crucially, however, for players who have never heard of the *Dune* universe outside of the game, it is the other way around. Located somewhere between fan-film and ersatz, direct-to-video sequels, as well as the Dune games being so important to game history itself, these scenes in *Dune 2000* in particular work unlike anything else in the constellation of the movie's tie-in products. They extend the visual language of the production, reinforcing the images from the 1984 film just two years before the universe would be re-imagined for television on the Sci-Fi Network.

The design of some elements in *Dune 2000* – such as the Atreides ornithoper craft – were more reminiscent of the work of John Schoenheer, the original illustrator for Herbert's novel. The sequel, *Emperor: Battle for Dune* extended the already dimly-connected plot and continued the real-time strategy gameplay format that had proven so successful in the preceding game. More designs and elements from the Lynch film were translated to this medium: the static, much-mocked Guild 'heighliners' of the film now rendered in the peculiar CGI style of action videogames, the red-haired Harkonnen boys belching threats at each other, the furry eyebrows of the Mentats twitching all the while.

These games extend the life of Lynch's *Dune* in an obvious way – they amplified its visual language, ideas and structure by repetition for a different audience. But they also extend the fictive *capacity* of the science fiction elements of *Dune*; despite their non-canonical status in terms of the strict parameters set by the rigid structures established by a dedicated fan base, they provide fascinating evidence of what the film *could* have been. The games, therefore, can be understood from this perspective almost as a kind of notetaking in the margin, but again more concretely are explicitly a vernacular and celebratory paratext. More than a tie-in or merchandising product, but less than a sequel, the *Dune* games are little fever dreams made possible by the intoxicating effects of the richness of the film, and the book in turn.

Footnotes

29. Many thanks to Dr. Brandum who provided this and further information in a thorough report exclusively for this book in January 2018.

5. THE GOLDEN PATH

Dune persists. With so many keen to disavow it, perhaps Lynch's film has a purpose and place as an unusual creature made in an unusual time, and one that appeals to unusual people. If the orthodoxies of film studies, Lynch critics and science fiction fans all wince and look away, then perhaps it explains why some iconoclasts have it buried deep in their psyche. For example, irascible continental philosopher Slavoj Žižek is obsessed with Lynch's *Dune*, and says 'it is his neglected masterpiece, with genuine moments of breathtaking poetic beauty' and that politically, he thinks it is time for the Left 'to appropriate a few key elements of Fascist ideology-like military heorism and the spirit of collective sacrifice' (2006: 13). This link between fascism, media and Lynch's *Dune* was not a new revelation to Žižek: a decade earlier, he noted 'Did you notice the use of multiple inner monologues? Reality is something very fragile for Lynch. If you get too close to it you discover Leni Riefenstahl' (Lovink 1996). Elsewhere, a passage in his book *The Metastates of Enjoyment* connects the inner voices of *Dune* to the cracking, leaking skulls of the Guildsman, and the eruptions of bodies hinted at throughout (1994: 116). His long essay on *Lost Highway*, 'The Art of the Ridiculous Sublime', discusses *Dune* several times in similar terms, again focusing on voice, narration, male power and dirty messiahs. (2000). Elsewhere, Žižek mentions *Dune* – again – in reference to Wagner's *Der Ring des Nibelungen* (*The Ring Cycle*). And in reference to Batman. And so on.

Žižek's obsession with *Dune* underlines a common theme among the fans of Lynch's film: having a strong reaction to it is like finding beauty in an unfinished puzzle. The reputation of its production aside, the sense that there are pieces missing in many ways makes the film stronger as there's an implication that there's more narrative to discover, more images to see, more intensity to feel. All this is in stark contrast to the finality of the film's ending, a total annihilation of the desert setting by cleansing rain. We are pulled in and can't escape.

Dune is always available to be speculated on because it itself is a kind of speculation. What *else* could science fiction be? The film's setting was sieved through the mind of a visual thinker like Lynch and structured purposefully like a house of cards in mid-collapse, or a poem with gaps in the middle of stanzas. Others have made similar interpretations: Daniel Snyder notes that the film is 'hinting at a greater, hidden story' (2014).

John DeVore is unabashedly fannish, talking about his favourite childhood toy sandworm, and how he would 'let heroes ride him but only if they had true hearts' (2017). But even this overtly subjective response to *Dune* implies that he too is drawn by this unspoken desire to look for answers, and he attempts to excuse the film's reception by stating that 'This movie was made by an outsider for insiders who then exiled the outsider once the money and praise didn't roll in' (2017). Lynch, of course, was never really exiled, yet as part of the ongoing myth-making around the film, this story is continually re-told and re-imagined – speculations on a speculative film. *Dune* is a story about myth-making at its heart; a warning shot over the bow of science fiction that has always bordered on being misunderstood, messy and gothic and alluring long before Lynch agreed to direct it, as demonstrated nowhere more visibly perhaps than in *Jodorowsky's Dune*. The promise in Herbert's *Dune* of social and political complexity through an ecological and psychosexual narrative gambit seems to hypnotise producers to line themselves up for an impossible task. The 2000 Sci-Fi Channel miniseries *Frank Herbert's Dune*, and its follow-up *Children of Dune*, are often considered more accurate but less charismatic than the film; a paradox which only heightened the attraction to Lynch's film for genre fans looking for answers.

Denis Villeneuve's insistence that his attempt to visit the *Dune* universe would move far away from Lynch is almost an unnecessary statement. The science fiction landscape today aches with pixel-perfect art direction, internationalised distribution systems, and it's where all the specialisation and production pipelines that were just germinating in 1984 have now overgrown to dominate every arena. There is no escape from the shadow of *Star Wars*, as Villeneuve discovered with the comparatively muted box office return for his *Blade Runner 2049* (2017).

Villeneuve's *Dune* appeared to have progressed through the same stages of traumatic growth in the pre-production phase as Lynch's; what was one film is rumoured at the time of writing to be two (Ruimy 2018). The novel contained many jumps in time that were refracted and translated by the 1984 film into its unique temporal structure, but Villeneuve's approach to temporal shifts in both *Arrival* and *Blade Runner 2049* demonstrate he has already tampered with timelines to great success. In *Polytechnique* (2009) and *Enemy* (2013), Villeneuve's broader capacity for intensity-in-motion was limitless. If *Dune* is approached with the same sleek visuality and confrontational emotional range as the director's impressive filmography up until now, it likely will be a version of the universe with little need to include the dense lingo and politicking that seemed so important in the 1980s. The new *Dune*, like the last, will appear a year after the conclusion of a *Star Wars* trilogy, but also a dominant quasi-science fiction Marvel film series around which other Hollywood films are now compared. If it succeeds, it is inevitable that Lynch's version will come under renewed scrutiny – perhaps the full-blown reassessment that *Newsweek*'s David Ansen called for.

The story of Lynch's *Dune* is still, then, being told. Some questions will continue to be sources of debate – unlikely to be addressed by Lynch himself. He is still asked the same question about *Dune* that he was in 1984: what did you learn? What do you wish you'd done differently? Why science fiction? The answers have remained steadily the same: always have final cut; I wish I'd said 'no'; I saw something promising. But the longevity and endurance of *Dune* alone indicates that at stake is much more than just questions about Lynch himself as a director: the film is a bridge between worlds and aesthetics. It folded space for us between a science fiction of our fitful youth and the world of incandescent immutable strangeness in art and auteur cinema. Lynch's *Dune* was a gateway drug to the infinite possibilities beyond; an adulteration of big budget, high concept cinema that required of you a little more than its peers with its fleeting intensities and moments of disgust, both working with the film and against it. *Dune* offered – and still does – a taste of something alien, unpleasant and powerful.

THE END

BIBLIOGRAPHY

Attanasio, P. (1984) 'Dune: Lost in the Dust'. *Washington Post* 14 December, C1+C4

Barney, R.A. (2009) *David Lynch: Interviews.* Jackson, University Press of Mississippi

Baumann, H. (2007) *Moebius Redux: A Life in Pictures* [online] available from <http://www.imdb.com/title/tt1029340/> [Accessed 21 February 2018]

Baxter, J. (1984) 'A Visual Dune Brings Science Fiction Down To Earth'. *Vogue* (December), 89

Belletto, S. and Grausam, D. (2012) *American Literature and Culture in an Age of Cold War: A Critical Reassessment.* Iowa City, University of Iowa Press

Berryman, J. (2000) *A Sting in the Tale.* Gateshead, Mirage Publishing

Biga, T. (1987) 'Review of Blue Velvet'. *Film Quarterly* 41 (1), 44–49

Braddock, J. and Hock, S. (2001) *Directed by Allen Smithee.* Minneapolis, MN, University of Minnesota Press

Breskin, D. (1997) *Inner Views: Filmmakers in Conversation.* Perseus Books Group

Broderick, D. (2003) 'New Wave and Backwash - 1960-1980'. in *The Cambridge Companion to Science Fiction.* Cambridge, Cambridge University Press, 48–63

Burgess, J. and Green, J. (2013) *YouTube: Online Video and Participatory Culture.* Oxford, John Wiley & Sons

Burt, C. (2014) *Anniversary of the Great Cold Wave of January 21, 1985 | Weather Extremes* [online] available from <https://www.wunderground.com/blog/weatherhistorian/anniversary-of-the-great-cold-wave-of-january-21-1985.html> [Accessed 27 March 2018]

Chion, M. (2005) *David Lynch.* London, BFI Publishing

Collins, B. (1985) 'Sci-Fi Epic Is Not To Be Missed'. *Daily Mirror* 9 July

Collins, W. (n.d.) *The Secret History of Dune* [online] available from <https://lareviewofbooks.org/article/the-secret-history-of-dune/> [Accessed 13 February 2018]

Consalvo, M. (2009) *Cheating: Gaining Advantage in Videogames.* Cambridge, MA, MIT Press

Crafts, F. (1977) 'Should Sci-Fi Author Sue?' *Eugene Register-Guard* 1 December

David Foster Wallace (1996) 'David Lynch Keeps His Head'. *Premiere* 10 (1), 90-95,108-110,112-114

Davis, S.O. (1984) 'Close Shaves on Set and In The Kitchen'. *Weekend Australian* 22 October, 59–60

Dean, J.F. (1978) 'Between 2001 and Star Wars'. *Journal of Popular Film and Television* 7 (1), 32–41

Debruge, P. (2013) 'Cannes Film Review: "Jodorowsky's Dune"'. [19 May 2013] available from <http://variety.com/2013/film/reviews/cannes-film-review-jodorowskys-dune-1200483641/> [Accessed 11 February 2018]

DeVore, J. (2017) *'Dune' Is 'Star Wars' For Goths* [online] available from <https://decider.com/2017/06/23/dune-david-lynch-john-devore/> [Accessed 9 February 2018]

Ebert, R. (1984) 'Dune: Review'. *Chicago Sun-Times* 1 January

Ellison, H. (1985) 'Dune'. *The Magazine of Fantasy and Science Fiction*

Fischer, D. (1985) 'Dune: Master Villian, The Baron Harkonnen'. *Enterprise Incidents* March, 27, 30–33

Francis, F. (2013) *Freddie Francis: The Straight Story from Moby Dick to Glory, a Memoir.* Lanham, Maryland, Scarecrow Press

Friendly, D.T. (1986) 'Another De Laurentiis Produces'. *Los Angeles Times* [online] 9 October. available from <http://articles.latimes.com/1986-10-09/entertainment/ca-5384_1_raffaella-de-laurentiis> [Accessed 31 March 2018]

Gallagher, C. (n.d.) *How 'Twin Peaks' Is Failing Its Female Characters* [online] available from <https://www.bustle.com/p/the-brutal-treatment-of-women-on-twin-peaks-strips-away-some-of-its-charm-61204> [Accessed 16 April 2018]

Gaylard, G. (2010) 'Postcolonial Science Fiction: The Desert Planet'. in *Science Fiction, Imperialism and the Third World: Essays on Postcolonial Literature and Film.* ed. by Sarwal, R. and Hoagland, E. Jefferson, NC, McFarland & Company

Godwin, K.G. (2016) *Dune: The David Lynch Files Volume 2.* British Columbia, Leanpub

Grazier, K. (2009) *The Science of Dune: An Unauthorized Exploration into the Real Science Behind Frank Herbert's Fictional Universe.* Dallas, BenBella Books Inc.

Haidenbauer, J. (n.d.) *Brian Eno Video/Web/Television* [online] available from <http://music.hyperreal.org/artists/brian_eno/videoother.html>

Har'el, A. (2008) *Paul Smith: The Reddest Herring* [online] available from <http://www.imdb.com/title/tt1381284/> [Accessed 20 March 2018]

Harmetz, A. (1983a) 'The World of 'Dune Is Filmed in Mexico'. *The New York Times* 4 September

Harmetz, A. (1983b) 'Dune: An Ordeal In The Mexican Desert'. *San Francisco Examiner-Chronicle* 25 September, 23

Hattenstone, S. (2007) *Simon Hattenstone Talks to David Lynch* [online] available from <http://www.theguardian.com/film/2007/feb/24/davidlynch> [Accessed 15 April 2018]

Herbert, F. (1987) *The Maker of Dune: Insights of a Master of Science Fiction.* New York, NY, Berkley Books

Herbert, F. (1985) *Eye.* New York, NY, Berkley Books

Herbert, F. (1980) 'Dune Genesis'. *Omni* July, 72–74

Herbert, F. (1965) *Dune*. Philadelphia, Chilton Books

Herbert, F. (2010) *Dune* (S.F. Masterworks). London, Orion Publishing.

Hoberek, A. (2012) 'Dune, The Middle Class, and Post-1960 U.S. Foreign Policy'. in *American Literature and Culture in an Age of Cold War: A Critical Reassessment*. ed. by Belletto, S. and Grausam, D. Iowa City, University of Iowa Press, 85–108

Hoberman, J. (1991) *Vulgar Modernism: Writing on Movies and Other Media*. Philadelphia, PA, Temple University Press

Hoberman, J. (1984) 'The End of Science Fiction'. *The Village Voice* (December 25), 67–68

Hodenfield, C. (1984) 'Daring Dune'. *Rolling Stone* 6 December, (436), 26–28

Hughes, D. (2014) *The Complete Lynch*. New York, NY, Random House

Ichbiah, D. (2017) *La Saga des Jeux Vidéo*. Daniel Ichbiah

Ismailos, A. (2010) *Great Directors* [online] available from <http://www.imdb.com/title/tt1445683/> [Accessed 1 April 2018]

James, E. and Mendlesohn, F. (2003) *The Cambridge Companion to Science Fiction*. Cambridge, Cambridge University Press

Jousse, T. (2010) *Masters of Cinema: David Lynch*. London, Phaidon Press

Kael, P. (74, 77-78) 'The Current Cinema: David and Goliath'. *The Village Voice* (December 24, 1984)

Kaleta, K.C. (1993) *David Lynch*. Michigan, Twayne Publishers

King, G. and Krzywinska, T. (2000) *Science Fiction Cinema: From Outerspace to Cyberspace*. London, Wallflower Press

Kuhn, A. (ed.) (1999) *Alien Zone II: The Spaces of Science-Fiction Cinema*. London, Verso

Kuhn, A. (1990) *Alien Zone: Cultural Theory and Contemporary Science Fiction Cinema*. London, Verso

Kunzru, H. (2015) *Dune, 50 Years on: How a Science Fiction Novel Changed the World* [online] available from <http://www.theguardian.com/books/2015/jul/03/dune-50-years-on-science-fiction-novel-world> [Accessed 13 February 2018]

Landon, B. (1999) 'Diegetic or Digital: The Convergence of Science-Fiction Film and Literature in Hypermedia'. in *Alien Zone II: The Spaces of Science-Fiction Cinema*. London, Verso

Landon, B. (1992) *The Aesthetics of Ambivalence: Rethinking Science Fiction Film in the Age of Electronic (Re)Production*. Westport, CT, Greenwood Press

LeGuin, U.K. (2016a) 'A Non-Euclidean View of California As A Cold Place To Be'. In More, T. *Utopia*. London, Verso

LeGuin, U.K. (2016b) 'Utopiyin/Utopiyang'. In More, T. *Utopia*. London, Verso

Lewis, B. (1985) 'The Creators of Dune'. *Films* January, 5 (1)

Lim, D. (2015) *David Lynch: The Man from Another Place*. Boston, MA, Houghton Mifflin Harcourt

Lofficier, R. and Lofficier, J.-M. (1985) 'Dean Stockwell - The Traitor of Dune'. *Starlog* January, 8 (90), 34-36, 65

Lovink, G. (1996) 'Civil Society, Fanaticism, and Digital Reality: A Conversation with Slavoj Zizek'. *CTheory* 0 (0), 2-21/1996

Lowry, B. (1984) '"Nick Castle: 'How Do You Get Around Star Wars?'"' *Starlog* (October), 62-65

Lynch, D. (2006) *Dune: Extended Edition*. [DVD] Universal

Lynch, D. (2004) *Dune: Special Edition*. [DVD] Universal / Sanctuary

Lynch, D. (2001) *'Eraserhead' Stories*.

Lynch, D. and Herbert, F. (1983) *Dune: A Recorded Interview*.

Mactaggart, A. (2010) *The Film Paintings of David Lynch: Challenging Film Theory*. Bristol, Intellect Books

Mandell, P. (1984a) 'David Lynch: Bewitched by the Bizarre'. *Starlog* (October), 49

Mandell, P. (1984b) 'David Lynch: Director of Dune'. *Starlog* (October), 46-48, 59

McGowan, T. (2007) *The Impossible David Lynch*. New York, NY, Columbia University Press

More, T. (2016) *Utopia*. London, Verso

Naha, E. (1984) *The Making of Dune*. New York, NY, Berkley Books

Ndalianis, A. (2011) *Science Fiction Experiences*. New Academia Publishing, LLC

Ndalianis, A. (2004) *Neo-Baroque Aesthetics and Contemporary Entertainment*. Cambridge, MA, MIT Press

Nieland, J. (2012) *David Lynch*. Champaign, IL, University of Illinois Press

Nochimson, M. (2014) *David Lynch Swerves: Uncertainty from Lost Highway to Inland Empire*. Austin, TX, University of Texas Press

Nochimson, M.P. (1997) *The Passion of David Lynch: Wild at Heart in Hollywood*. Austin, TX, University of Texas Press

Odell, C. and Blanc, M.L. (2007) *David Lynch*. Harpenden, Oldcastle Books

O'Hanlon, T. (1984) 'The First Billion-Dollar Flick?' *Forbes Magazine* 5 November, 64-66, 70-71

Olson, G. (2008) *David Lynch: Beautiful Dark*. Lanham, Maryland, Scarecrow Press

O'Mahony, J. (2002) *The Guardian Profile: David Lynch* [online] available from <http://www.theguardian.com/film/2002/jan/12/awardsandprizes.books> [Accessed 15 April 2018]

O'Reilly, T. (1981) *Frank Herbert*. New York, NY, Frederick Ungar Publishing

Pollock, D. (1984) 'Is Dune Doomed to Financial Wasteland?' *San Francisco Sunday Examiner & Chronicle* 23 December

Prucher, J. (2007) *Brave New Words: The Oxford Dictionary of Science Fiction*. Oxford, Oxford University Press

Rehak, B. (2018) *More Than Meets the Eye: Special Effects and the Fantastic Transmedia Franchise*. New York, NY, NYU Press

Richards, L.L. (2000) *Interview | Brian Herbert and Kevin J. Anderson* [online] available from <http://www.januarymagazine.com/profiles/duneprofile.html> [Accessed 9 February 2018]

Rickman, G. (1993a) 'Review: By Any Means Necessary: The Trials and Tribulations of the Making of "Malcolm X" by Spike Lee, Ralph Wiley'. *FILM QUART* 46 (4), 64-64

Rickman, G. (1993b) 'Review: The Aesthetics of Ambivalence: Re-Thinking Science Fiction Film in the Age of Electronic (Re)Production by Brooks Landon'. *FILM QUART* 46 (4), 63-64

Rovner, S. (1981) 'The Myth-Master of Dune'. *Washington Post* [online] 24 April. available from <https://www.washingtonpost.com/archive/lifestyle/1981/05/24/the-myth-master-of-dune/c2c71c7f-bf09-4a6b-b479-263bf9eb1579/> [Accessed 12 February 2018]

Ruimy, J. (n.d.) *Director Denis Villeneuve Says 'Dune' Will Be At Least Two Films* [online] available from <https://theplaylist.net/denis-villeneuve-two-dune-films-20180309/> [Accessed 28 March 2018]

Sammon, P. (1984) 'My Year on Arrakis: A "Dune" Diary'. *Cinefantastique* 14 (4-5), 28-40, 73-91

Sammon, P.M. (1999) *Ridley Scott: Close Up: The Making of His Movies*. Boston, MA, Da Capo Press

Sapp, K. (2014) *Students Fight Invasive Plants to Restore Oregon Dunes*. Available from <https://www.usda.gov/media/blog/2014/05/29/students-fight-invasive-plants-restore-oregon-dunes> [Accessed 29 May 2014]

Schneller, J. (1992) 'The Secret World of Kyle MacLachlan'. *GQ* August, 62 (134-137, 197)

Schwarz, J. (2002) *Mysteries of Love* [online] available from <http://www.imdb.com/title/tt0312988/> [Accessed 24 February 2018]

Sheen, E. (2004) 'Going Into Strange Worlds: David Lynch, Dune and New Hollywood'. In *The Cinema of David Lynch: American Dreams, Nightmare Visions*. London, Wallflower Press

Sheen, E. and Davison, A. (2004) *The Cinema of David Lynch: American Dreams, Nightmare Visions*. Wallflower Press

Sibley, A. (2001) *Dino De Laurentiis: The Last Movie Mogul* [online] available from <http://www.imdb.com/title/tt0327642/> [Accessed 20 March 2018]

Snyder, D.D. (2014) 'The Messy, Misunderstood Glory of David Lynch's Dune'. *The Atlantic* [online] 14 March. available from <https://www.theatlantic.com/entertainment/archive/2014/03/the-messy-misunderstood-glory-of-david-lynchs-em-dune-em/284316/> [Accessed 11 February 2018]

Sobchack, V.C. (1987) *Screening Space: The American Science Fiction Film*. New Brunswick, NJ, Rutgers University Press

Strauss, R. (1984) 'Raffaella De Laurentiis'. *Enterprise Incidents* December, 7–8

Strick, P. (2001) 'Riddle of the Sands'. *Sight and Sound* 11 (9), 20–22

The Guardian Lectures: David Lynch (1985) RPM Productions / Channel 4

Todd, A. (2012) *Authorship and the Films of David Lynch: Aesthetic Receptions in Contemporary Hollywood*. London, I.B. Tauris

Turner, P. (1973) 'Interview with Frank Herbert'. *Vertex* October, 1 (4), 34–38

Turnock, J.A. (2014) *Plastic Reality: Special Effects, Technology, and the Emergence of 1970s Blockbuster Aesthetics*. New York, NY, Columbia University Press

Wallace, D.F. (2012) *A Supposedly Fun Thing I'll Never Do Again*. London, Hachette UK

Wood, R. (1986) *Hollywood From Vietnam to Reagan*. New York, NY, Columbia University Press

Woodward, R.B. (1990) 'A Dark Lens on America'. *The New York Times* [online] 14 January. available from <http://www.nytimes.com/1990/01/14/magazine/a-dark-lens-on-america.html> [Accessed 24 February 2018]

Yahoo! (n.d.) *Blade Runner 2049 Director Denis Villeneuve* [online] available from <https://www.facebook.com/yahooentertainment/videos/10156818808494832/>

Žižek, S. (2006) 'Guilty Pleasures'. *Film Comment*; New York 42 (1), 12–13

Žižek, S. (2005) *The Metastases of Enjoyment: Six Essays on Women and Causality*. London, Verso

Žižek, S. (2000a) *The Art of the Ridiculous Sublime: On David Lynch's Lost Highway*. Seattle, WA, Walter Chapin Simpson Center for the Humanities, University of Washington

Žižek, S. (2000b) *The Ticklish Subject: The Absent Centre of Political Ontology*. London, Verso

www.ingramcontent.com/pod-product-compliance
Ingram Content Group UK Ltd.
Pitfield, Milton Keynes, MK11 3LW, UK
UKHW021557230326
469232UK00007B/211